A SONG OF FORGIVENESS

By the same author:

Hands Free of Violence

A
Song of
Forgiveness

J. ERIC MAYER

KINGSWAY PUBLICATIONS
EASTBOURNE

Unless otherwise indicated, biblical quotations are from
the Holy Bible: New International Version,
copyright © International Bible Society 1973, 1978, 1984.

Front cover photo: Tony Stone Photolibrary—London

British Library Cataloguing in Publication Data

Mayer, J. Eric (James Eric), *1923–*
A song of forgiveness.
1. Christian life. Forgiveness
I. Title
248.4

ISBN 0 86065 516 4

Printed in Great Britain for
KINGSWAY PUBLICATIONS LTD
Lottbridge Drove, Eastbourne, E. Sussex BN23 6NT by
Cox & Wyman Ltd, Reading, Berks.
Typeset by Nuprint Ltd, Harpenden, Herts AL5 4SE.

Contents

Acknowledgements

With grateful thanks to Miss Bernie O'Rourke who so cheerfully and willingly typed out the final manuscript, making the writing of the book so much easier.

Also to the Community of the Christian Renewal Centre, Rostrevor, Co. Down who released me from Community duties while the book was being written.

Preface

It puzzled me why God should want to hear a new song coming from the hearts of his people. Eight times the Bible exhorts us to sing a new song to the Lord. The new song must be important to the Lord to cause him to mention it in his word so many times. I wondered what the new song would sound like.

In Sunday worship many of us sing the old songs, written in the eighteenth and nineteenth centuries. In renewal circles we sing the new songs, the ones that are being composed today. They are coming in such large numbers and so rapidly that we are all resorting to overhead projectors instead of song books so that the new ones can be added easily as they are composed.

I like the songs we sing, both old and new, but I know they are not the ones to which the Lord refers when he sends out the call: 'Sing to the Lord a new song.' I wondered whether I would recognize such a song if I ever heard it.

Then one day I heard the new song. It was beautiful. I knew instantly that the Lord would be thrilled to hear it. It came from the heart of the singer and it was just the sound for which the Lord had been waiting.

I heard it first in Northern Ireland, the last place on this earth from which I would have expected such a glorious sound to come. For centuries Ireland has been dogged by its history. The Irish people, North and South, feed on the past. They celebrate past events with parades, flags and emotional speeches. Whether it is the potato famine, the Battle of the Boyne or the 1916 Rising, it has to be remembered. There is no forgiveness for the past in Ireland. The hurts go too deep and the memories are sharpened for each new generation that comes along.

Then I sat down in Rostrevor where Percy French got the inspiration for his song: 'Where the mountains of Mourne sweep down to the sea,' and I heard the new song. I had never thought the day would come when I would hear such a song being sung in Ireland. I went to Belfast and heard it again. Then to London, where it was filling the air of that busy city.

They were singing, 'I forgive...and I will remember your sin no more.'

Introduction

The first three chapters in this study of the subject of forgiveness are made up of three separate true stories of people who have been able to forgive under exceptionally difficult circumstances. They stand as separate entities with no attempt being made to link them in any way.

As you go on to read how the theme of forgiveness runs right through the Bible I trust that you will be able to see how those three stories illustrate the truth of what the Bible is teaching.

This pattern is followed right through the book—stories from life, illustrating how the biblical teaching works out in practice. It is hoped that this will be an encouragement to all readers to allow those same principles to be worked out practically in their own lives.

I

A Tit-For-Tat Killing

It was a dark wet evening in Belfast, Northern Ireland. The street was deserted when a car pulled up outside a large, ancient Congregational church building. A young attractive girl jumped out of the driving seat and bent down to lock the car door before running into the church. She was putting the key into the lock when a man stepped out of the shadows behind her and said: 'I am going to kill you.'

The girl laughed. It must be someone from the church youth group trying to be funny. The silent September night was violated by the crack of a pistol as the bullet tore through the girl's neck. She fell to the ground—still laughing.

Twenty-year-old Karen McKeown had started on a three-week fight to save her life—an almost hopeless battle to restore a body that was paralysed from the neck down. The bullet, located later by the police, had severed her spinal chord.

As Karen's body hit the road her watch, a present from her boyfriend, stopped at 8.20 p.m. It was Saturday, 25th September 1982 and an hour earlier the now silent church had been filled with singing to welcome the installation of its new minister, the Rev. Ken Finlay. Those who had been left to do the tidying and washing up had stopped in their tracks at the sound of the shot. Not everyone was sure what had made the noise. There was always the hope that it could be a car back-firing, but in Northern Ireland the possibility of a rifle shot is never far from anyone's mind. A few people ran out into the street to investigate.

Soon Karen was surrounded by caring people. An umbrella was sheltering her from the rain. A blanket kept her warm until the ambulance arrived. Her home for the next three weeks was the intensive care unit of the Royal Victoria Hospital, and every second of her existence depended upon a life-support machine.

Two friends went to Karen's home to tell her parents, John and Pearl, the truth—but not the whole truth. They told them that Karen had been found lying beside her car and she had been taken to hospital. Pearl with the active mind of a nursing assistant quickly worked out what must have happened. She knew that one of Karen's contact lenses had blown away in the wind recently. If this had happened again she might not have been able to see clearly as she stepped out of the car on a dark night. She could easily have slipped, fallen and knocked herself out momentarily.

At the hospital someone tried to tell Pearl a different story; that a man had shot Karen in an attempt to murder her, but that was too ludicrous for any mother to believe. Who in the whole wide world could possibly want to murder her lovely daughter? The idea was so ridiculous that Pearl's mind rejected it completely.

Why, Karen had sung so beautifully in church that evening, looking lovely in her white jumper and skirt, her brown eyes sparkling with life, her hair, about which she was so particular, neatly set to show off its brown sheen. Then she drove her mother home in the car, bubbling over with high spirits all the way, to the extent that Pearl's protective instincts warned Karen to drive more carefully, as she did not even seem to be looking where she was going.

The original intention was that Pearl would help to clear

12

up after the service, but she had worked hard as a nurse as well as getting the supper ready and was tired so Karen volunteered to do the tidying up for her and drove her mother home. Then she returned to the church.

No one could possibly have a motive for shooting a girl like Karen, so Pearl sat in the intensive care unit and told Karen that she had fallen and hurt her head. This did not please the radiologist in charge of the case. He insisted that Karen must be told the truth. So it was he who broke the news to Karen as she lay unable to move any part of her body except her head. She cried quietly for a while as her mind absorbed this horrible truth.

Karen could not breathe except for the help of a life-support machine. At first she was unable to speak, but when a tube was removed from her throat she could whisper and mouth words. Her family quickly learned to understand what she was saying. Her heart was constantly being monitored, and tubes ran into her arm—one feeding her, and another supplying morphine to bring relief from pain.

Pearl felt so helpless beside her daughter in such circumstances. Somehow she tried to convey love and strength to that helpless figure that had once been so active and had stood in Buckingham Palace with her best friend as they both received the Duke of Edinburgh's gold medal for achievement. A gospel singer, a sub-officer in the Girl's Brigade, a student in her final year at Queen's University, Belfast and a part-time librarian (who in that way earned enough money to run her own car). Now she lay so helpless.

John, a driving instructor, was glad when his daughter had passed her test. It was hard to watch her now, but those three weeks at her bedside changed his life completely. Karen's Christian faith never wavered for a moment, her face was so often radiant, she never expressed a word of bitterness or resentment. Never had a life spoken so deeply to him and in the course of those three weeks he told Karen that he had taken the decision to dedicate his life to the Lord and to become a Christian. Karen did not have to make any response. Her face registered all the joy she felt. 'But I don't know what to do next,' said John. 'Daddy, you just trust,' said Karen as she expressed the moment-by-moment experience that she was living through. There was nothing she could do but trust the Lord each moment of the day.

Pearl was a little apprehensive when she heard that her husband had committed his life to the Lord. She hoped he was not trying to make some kind of bargain with God (I'll give my life to you if you will heal my daughter). There was a growing conviction within Pearl that her daughter was going to die, and then what would happen to John's new-found faith? She need not have worried. John's faith has grown from strength to strength over the four years since his daughter died.

Karen's Christian commitment came when she was fourteen years of age. Neither of her parents were Christians then, but they understood the step she had taken. Karen's ambition was to be a Probation Officer, and that was what she was training for, but Pearl had misgivings there. Her daughter was too soft-hearted with both animals and people for the Probation service.

It was Karen's brother, Leslie, who was the first member of the family to become a Christian and it was he who had led Karen to the Lord. Brother and sister were very close and Leslie would have done anything for his sister. It was through him that one of the strangely ironic things in life happened. The first child to be born to Leslie and his wife arrived the day before Karen died. It was a little girl, Rebekah. Although this was her first grandchild, Pearl found her arrival at that time hard to take. If the Lord felt he was compensating her in some way for the loss of Karen, she wanted him to know that no one could ever make up for that loss. She did not want a grandchild. She wanted her daughter.

Rebekah, who is now four and has a two-year-old brother, David, had to take on the task of winning over her granny's love and acceptance. She did it quite simply, just by loving her granny and letting that love deepen more and more as she developed her own personality. Pearl loves her granddaughter now, but her first reaction was just one of the battles through which she had to win her way. She was greatly helped by her beautiful daughter-in-law, Vivien, who said, 'The Lord knew nine months ago we would need Rebekah.'

Karen had sung in a girls' quartet called Eldad (after an elder with a prophetic ministry in the days of Moses). Her best friend, Linda, was also a member, and she and Karen had also sung duets. Perhaps there was something prophetic in the songs they chose to sing. Pearl felt they were too young to be singing 'I'll fly away,' but it was one of the songs they enjoyed singing. On that fateful evening of the installation service Karen had sung 'I will enter his gates with thanksgiving'.

Linda is married to a policeman, and for a time Karen thought that Linda had been shot too. There might be some kind of twisted, distorted sense in gunmen aiming at the family of a Northern Ireland policeman. There seemed no sense at all in shooting Karen McKeown. The only way Karen could be convinced that Linda was all right was by making a special arrangement for Linda to go to the intensive care unit so that Karen could see her.

No one has ever been charged with Karen's murder. The bullet enabled the police to determine that the gun used was the same one as the INLA (Irish National Liberation Army) used to shoot a Councillor a year previously. Powder burns on Karen's jumper showed that she had been shot at close range. There were no witnesses to the shooting. A man was detained by the police on two seven-day special detention orders, but there was insufficient evidence for conviction.

With the tragic logic of Northern Ireland reasoning a motive was established. The night before Karen was shot a Catholic girl was shot and wounded on Short Strand, a street a few yards from Albert Bridge in Belfast where the River Lagan flows through the city, and a few yards from the church. It was a tit-for-tat shooting. A Protestant girl had to be shot as near to the scene of the first shooting as possible. All the gunman had to do was to wait outside a Protestant church until a girl went in or out on her own. The girl was Karen.

The church building has since been demolished to make way for a street-widening scheme and a new one erected nearby. The girls' quartet has been disbanded, too heart-broken to continue singing as a trio. Karen's life on earth has ended. She died at 8.10 p.m. on 16th October 1982. Her parents, brother and boyfriend Stephen are left to demonstrate to the church and the world that forgiveness even under those circumstances can be made possible by the Lord.

During those three weeks Stephen somehow held on to the hope that Karen would recover. It meant believing in a miracle, but as a Christian he never ruled out that possibility. Pearl knew Karen would die, but was so grateful for those three weeks in which to sit with her. If Karen had died instantly without any opportunity for goodbyes Pearl does not think she could have coped as she did.

People all over the world were praying for Karen in those traumatic three weeks. Normally gifts are not allowed into an intensive care unit but an exception was made in Karen's case. The room was inundated with cards and flowers. They stopped counting the cards after the first 200.

For Pearl those three weeks took on the character of a kind of unrealistic limbo experience. She couldn't remember buying any food, but every time she went home there was food there, and very often sandwiches or some other meal prepared. It was months later that Pearl discovered that a friend called Lily had looked after her home and kept it stocked with food. She became Pearl's closest friend. There was one other person, a male nurse, with whom Pearl was especially close. Those two friends meant a great deal to her. When they both died, within eighteen months of each other, one of them in great pain, it was almost more than Pearl could bear. She became really angry with God. She had born the sorrow of her daughter's tragic death without a trace of resentment against God, but for him to allow her closest friends to be taken as well was, it seemed to her, to be piling on more than anyone should be asked to bear.

At that time Pearl had begun to give her testimony at meetings, telling of the miracle that God had performed in her life enabling her to forgive the man who had killed her daughter, but there was no way in which she could speak of God's goodness in the face of the death of her two closest friends. She told the Lord she would never speak at a meeting again. There was one invitation outstanding that she had accepted, but she told the organizers that she would not be going. They pleaded with her to keep the appointment as they had publicized the meeting, so Pearl warned them that if she did go and speak she would tell the people exactly how she felt and how angry she was with God. They were prepared to take that risk so Pearl went, read from the Bible and then poured out her hurt and frustration with the Lord. It is doubtful if the people present had ever heard a talk like it and it was certainly not what you would expect to hear at a Christian meeting, but it was just what many needed to hear—a Christian honestly expressing her rebellion against what God was doing. The Lord used it to bless and encourage many who heard her that evening.

The deaths of those two friends, Arnold and Lily, one a Catholic and the other a Protestant, was as though the Lord had removed two crutches on which Pearl was leaning and depending. The Lord was showing her never to depend on anyone other than himself.

Pearl had never spoken at a public meeting before Karen died. The first occasion came without any warning and after that she received invitations from all over the country. Two years before Karen's death Pearl had felt that the Lord wanted her to become involved in the work of Prison Fellowship in Ireland, but she had no desire for that and did nothing about it. As Karen fought for her life, Pearl was shown a letter written from prison by a member of the INLA, the organization that owned the gun used to shoot Karen. The man was Liam McCloskey and the letter explained how he had become a Christian at the end of a fifty-five-day hunger strike in which he temporarily lost his sight and was near to death. Now that same man wrote saying that he and four other Christian prisoners were praying for Karen round the clock. They were in Magilligan Prison serving long sentences, and Liam had gone on hunger strike in a demand to be treated as a political prisoner rather than as a criminal. In his letter he told Pearl to read Isaiah 38:10, words that the Lord had used to change his life: 'In the prime of my life must I go through the gates of death and be robbed of the rest of my years?' Liam was rushing to his own self-inflicted death when he read those words and realized that no one and nothing was worth dying for except Jesus Christ.

Liam read on in that chapter and came to verse 14: 'My eyes grew weak as I looked to the heavens. I am troubled; O Lord, come to my aid!' Liam echoed that cry from his own heart, and that was the turning point in his life. The next day he read verse 16: 'You restored me to health and let me live.' Today Liam is out of prison testifying publicly to the greatness of God's forgiveness. Realizing how much God has forgiven him, Liam will say: 'How can we not forgive when the Lord forgives so much?'

This former member of the INLA was the man whom the Lord brought across Pearl's path. He now visits their home, and is the only person ever to be allowed to spend a night in what used to be Karen's bed.

Towards the end, Karen began suffering from headaches. This was the evidence of the meningitis which eventually caused her death. Every afternoon and evening some members of the family would sit with her. In the mornings the doctors and nurses took over the ward. When the family was there they did not talk about the shooting. If the subject did come up, Karen's response would always be: 'It doesn't matter, Mummy,' but there were always other more pleasant things to chat about, especially now that the whole family could talk about the Lord as the One who was with them through all of that time. One day Karen shrugged her paralysed shoulders and the family rushed to tell the good news to the doctor. Surely this was a sign of hope? Their hopes were dashed when they were told that it was only a reflex action.

There was nearly always music being played softly in the background. Karen liked to listen to Joni, the American girl who hit her head while diving into the sea and has had to spend the rest of her life in a wheelchair, paralysed from the neck down. Karen had read all of Joni's books, never dreaming that one day she too would be paralysed (except that Karen would never get into a wheelchair because of her need to be strapped to machines). In one of the books Joni tells of a certain vindictive night nurse who used to inflict unnecessary suffering. That chapter almost broke Karen's heart.

The Joni songs are never heard in the McKeown household today. Having heard them almost every day in hospital, Pearl finds that they arouse stronger emotions than she can cope with.

Also present in that hospital ward was Karen's Bible, given to her by Stephen's mother two years before the shooting. Pearl carries it with her wherever she goes so that people can see the underlined passages and the comments written neatly in the margins by Karen. For two years before her death Karen had studied the subject of unjust suffering, paying particular attention to the book of Job and covering it with her marginal comments. The comments were brief but very much to the point—'God incited the matter, not Satan'; 'The devil functions within God's purposes'. Karen's mind and faith were shaped around such thoughts as those. Even as she lay dying she knew that Satan had attacked her in that evil deed, but also that Satan could move only within the providence of a sovereign God who has promised that Christians will never be tested beyond what they are able to endure.

As a comment on Romans 3 she wrote: 'Faith begins where man's power ends.' The faith that began on the night the gun was fired was a different faith from that which had operated in the life of the family before. It was a gift of faith of a quality that Daniel must have known in the lions' den.

Leslie read to his sister every day from her Bible. Some passages were easier to read than others. It was often the underlined verses that were the hardest to read out loud; like Job 13:15—'Though he slay me, yet will I hope in him.'

When sitting beside the bed of her paralysed daughter Pearl's mind seemed to function in two ways at once. One half was concentrating on the conversation with Karen and what they would talk about next, but the other half was quietly working its way through all that was happening, thinking it through and trying to evaluate her reactions. How would she react if the man who fired the shot was ever caught? Her mind seemed to wrap itself round that question almost effortlessly and come up with an answer, as though it was the Lord and not her that was directing her thoughts. She decided that she would be glad that he was caught because at least then he would not be able to kill again. In prison he would have time to dwell on what he had done and perhaps a spirit of repentance might come to him and he would be able to experience the Lord's forgiveness. Pearl decided she would go and see him and tell him that she forgave him, and she would lend him Karen's Bible so that he could read her notes and discover something of the kind of girl she was. She would go back after a week to learn his reactions to what he had read.

Pearl's mind has worked through many questions of that kind. She has pictured the man with the gun in his hand—the devil and Christ standing beside him at that moment.

The man had a free will to choose for evil or for good, to kill or not to kill. Once he decided to kill he had reached the point of no return. He became the devil's tool, but he could just as easily have made the other choice and put the gun away. Pearl reckons that if Jesus had stepped in to change the man's mind and so prevent him from killing, the man would have become a robot and would have lost his free will. This helps her to realize that it was not God's will that Karen should be shot, that man does have the choice to go against God and to go the way of evil. Her husband, John, may not quite see it that way. He goes more on the line that nothing happens that is not God's will, but Pearl sees that the Lord will permit people to disobey him, even to the point of taking a life. She also sees how wonderfully the Lord can take man's evil deeds and bring good out of them.

Pearl knows that in her natural state she would have been all for taking a gun and going out for revenge. She says, 'You have to pour out all the hatred that may be in you and ask the Lord to empty you, and then to fill you with his love and forgiveness. It is like the line of a song we sometimes sing, "Make me like a precious stone, crystal clear and finely honed." This is what I pray for.'

Thinking back to the night of the shooting, Pearl realizes that there may have been girls in the church that evening who were not Christians. If they had been shot they would not have been ready to face the Lord. In Karen's case Pearl is convinced that the Lord had prepared her daughter. She sees the marked Bible as clear proof of that. Karen was no plaster saint. She was a modern young lady who loved dancing, music and fast driving, and she had all the faults and shortcomings of any girl, but she was prepared and ready for whatever the Lord wanted in her life. This made it easier for Pearl to let Karen go. Karen never portrayed the face of a victim in her suffering.

It was not often that Pearl was alone with Karen in the hospital as there was nearly always other members of the family present, but on one occasion there was just the two of them and Karen asked her mother to cream her hands for her. As Pearl rubbed on the cream Karen remarked that she was unable to feel anything at all. Then she added: 'But, it doesn't matter,' and soon afterwards she fell asleep. Pearl allowed herself to have a quiet cry, but Karen awoke and spotted the red eyes. She said: 'Mum, think of the mother of the man who did it. How must she feel?' Then she added: 'I am sorry he did it, but I am more sorry for him.' This was Karen's philosophy.

Karen's death was so peaceful, so quiet, that it was more like slipping away than dying. The Albert Bridge Accordion Band had sent a massive cake that had been baked to mark their silver jubilee. Karen saw it and it brought a smile to her face. It was then handed over to the hospital staff for them to eat.

Karen always liked her hair to look nice so she asked her mother to wash it for her. Before this was done she mentioned that she had a headache. Afterwards she settled down to rest. Those were the last words she spoke. She slipped into a sleep and was gone.

Among the hundreds of letters of sympathy was one from the Duke of Edinburgh who remembered her as a winner of the gold medal award in the scheme that he inaugurated.

On the day of the funeral Pearl got ready for the church service and automatically put on a black suit. As she came downstairs and looked at what she was wearing, she went back upstairs and changed into a blue skirt and white blouse. She felt certain that was what Karen would have wanted. It is the custom in Northern Ireland for relations to carry the coffin at least part of the way along the road between the church and the burial ground, and so the relations never doubted that this would happen with Karen's coffin, but Pearl had a problem with this. Karen had once watched on television the funeral of a victim of the violence and she saw the coffin being carried down the street. She voiced her horror at this and said she hoped that no one would ever carry her coffin down the street. She recoiled at any kind of show, and this was too much of a public spectacle for her liking, so Pearl put her foot down and insisted that once the coffin was carried out of church it must be placed in the hearse. Not everyone understood that decision, but a mother must be allowed to obey the dictates of her own heart on such occasions.

The church was packed for the service. It seemed as though all of the Catholics from the Short Strand were in the service. The whole of that day was a strange sensation for Pearl. It was as though the Lord had built a wall around her so that she was completely protected from all that went on. Her only real recollection of the service was that she felt cold all over. Linda's husband, the policeman, told her at the end of the service that there were cameramen outside. He put his arm around her and rushed her out to a waiting car.

When she got back home the house was full of people and there was food prepared for them all, but she had not made any preparations. It was Lily again who had done it all. Pearl was still shielded from all reactions. It was like being at a buffet supper. She walked round and talked with everyone, feeling detached from the whole event. Such was the Lord's protection.

That is all in Pearl's past. Now she is coping with the present, involved with the work of Prison Fellowship, speaking at meetings and not always finding it easy. The message of forgiveness is a difficult one for many people to accept. She does not make notes or prepare talks. Her thoughts just spill out one after the other. It was the same when she talked with me. Once she had told her story the rest of her thoughts and memories came tumbling out just as she felt them.

'I remember speaking at Enniskillen and I felt hatred well up from the audience. It was as though someone in the audience was trying to put something evil on to me. I was ill afterwards. At other times I sense extreme bitterness radiating from the audience. I once read Martin Luther

23

King's speech on love but was told afterwards that you can carry that kind of teaching too far. People talk to me about God's wrath and retribution, but God has commanded me to forgive.

'I am an Irish Christian. I would never say I am a Protestant. That has become a dirty word. The conflict in Northern Ireland is a self-inflicted war. Even the children are being brainwashed and taught to say, 'Kick the Pope.' The demon of bigotry has got into the churches, but the people do not recognize that this is the cause of their bitterness. There is nothing to fear except fear itself.

'I do not know why the Lord took a rebel like me and gave me the gift of forgiveness. I offend the Lord over and over again. I could be going round as the most vindictive person in the world. It is only through God's grace that I am able to forgive so easily.'

That is Pearl McKeown's story.

The same evening after Karen was shot, Belfast police were called out to a second case. This time it was an elderly man and he was already dead. They found the bullet and put it alongside the one fired at Karen. They both came from the same gun. The man who pulled the trigger is in need of forgiveness from both God and man. His need is great, but God's forgiveness knows no bounds. Jesus still stands beside that man waiting for him to make the decision to turn from evil to Christ. The decision is his.

2

Response to the Brighton Bomb

It was on the 12th October, 1984 that a bomb, skillfully hidden by the IRA in a bedroom of the Grand Hotel at Brighton, exploded at the start of the annual Conservative Party Conference. Buried somewhere in the rubble were the Rt Hon. Sir Anthony Berry, Member of Parliament for Southgate in North London, and his second wife.

Waiting in a flat in London for news were Sir Anthony's twin daughters by his first marriage. With the telephone beside them and the television on continuously, it was an agonizing time. It was like drowning in a rough sea with little hope of anyone throwing in a lifeline. One of the sisters had been preparing to go to the school where she taught when the news of the explosion broke on TV. She woke her sister, Joanna, who was packed and ready to leave for Africa the next day. As they started their vigil Joanna had a strong premonition that her father would not survive the bomb.

He had originally booked into another hotel with his wife, but the day before the explosion he heard that there was a vacant room at the Grand and so they moved in there.

A son, Edward, was living in Brighton and he set out to search for news, phoning the sisters whenever he had any scrap of information. He knew his parents were staying at the Grand as he had supper with them there the previous evening. Sir Anthony's wife was rescued from under a pile of rubble, badly injured. She was rushed to hospital. By then Edward had discovered that there was no trace of their bedroom still remaining.

Rumours were flying. Someone told Edward that he had seen Sir Anthony. Could it be true?

Then came the news that a body had been recovered with a signet ring on one finger. Edward wore an identical ring so it was taken from him to see if they matched. It was in that time of waiting that hope began to recede fast.

The man returned with the news that the two rings matched. Once again the phone rang in the London flat with the sad news that ended the five hours of anxious waiting. Now the two children of the second marriage, both in boarding schools, had to be informed. The twin sisters drove to Eton where George, the eldest, was a pupil. The housemaster lent them his office in which to break the news. George took it stoically, as his father would have expected of him, without tears. Then came the journey to the next school to tell Sasha. There it was more difficult. No room was made available and they had to break the news in the school car park, with people milling around. It was no place to break sad news, or to bring comfort afterwards.

Joanna's planned visit to Africa was cancelled. She endured the cremation service, which was followed two weeks later by a private funeral which her step-mother managed to attend on crutches. Through it all the family had little privacy. The media were full of what had happened. It became a public event rather than a private grief. Each news bulletin was a reminder to the family of their tragedy.

Joanna was still trying to convince herself that her father was dead. Somehow she had to come to terms with this. Her own mother was in Africa, still recovering from the shock of her brother having shot himself some six weeks previously.

Joanna was twenty-seven years of age when her father

was killed. For eleven of those years she had been searching for answers to the many questions in her mind about the meaning of life, the vast problems to be found in the world and the purpose of her own existence. She had some answers. She had a strong faith in God and was committed to doing God's will, but did not know how to translate this into everyday life. This brought its own struggle and confusion. She now had the feeling that her father's tragic death would somehow provide the key that would unlock the door for her. Perhaps it was through such devastating experience that she would find the answers for which she was still looking.

It was while she was still at school, around the age of fourteen, that Joanna decided she would not find the answers she needed simply by conforming to the set patterns of life laid down for her by the society in which she lived. Her parents had divorced when she was six, which had already upset part of the pattern. She was brought up by her mother, with times fixed by a court when she was to see her father. That mode of life could quickly have formed its own pattern for her, but she began to break out of the mould in her own way by playing truant from school. Often she would go to school in time for registration and then slip out without being noticed.

She saw this rebellion as a time of exploration. She had a thirst to find out things, to be a discoverer, to experiment. She kept diaries to record her experiences and they became full of unanswered questions.

There was a sense in which she was being self-destructive without realizing it. She tried Marijuana because everyone was using it. She studied psychology and did a vast amount of reading and listening. The problem was that her mind was filling with negative thoughts instead of the positive answers she needed. She thought of herself as being evil. She was convinced that God had left her and had no further interest in her. She became more and more confused, but from her outward appearance and demeanour she seemed to be confident, full of life, and happy. Despite all the missed time at school she managed to scrape through her exams. It was a deception that fooled everyone except herself.

At seventeen she met a man with whom she lived for six years. She never felt she had any choice in the matter. Alan had a strange power over her, especially in his more depressive moods, and there seemed no way in which she could have broken off the relationship. He would threaten to kill himself if she spoke of leaving and emotional blackmail of that kind is very powerful. She accepted the situation, even though it was a cause of grief to her parents, and saw it as a further time of exploration and learning.

They went to Mexico together and she visited a friend of her mother's. They built up a good relationship. The friend seemed to understand Joanna and to accept her as she was rather than trying to change her.

At this time Joanna became very ill with a high fever and lapsed into delirium. It looked as though she was dying and she had the sensation of leaving her body as though to enter another world. She was given a choice, either to remain out of her body or to return and take up her life on earth again. She chose to return but did so with the sense that God had not deserted her after all.

This was a turning point for Joanna and one in which her health began to return. She began to see life in a more positive way. She no longer felt herself to be the victim of circumstances. She began meeting the right people; people who were able to help her. Even an old man she helped across a busy street gave her some sound advice.

She was still living with Alan and together they went to India. Her mind was now accepting that she was going to have to leave him, but she knew that this would not be easy. It was hot and sticky in Delhi during the monsoon season and their money was running out. Joanna wanted to go into the mountains to stay with Tibetan refugees she knew were living there. Alan wanted to return to England so they parted, although it was meant to be only a temporary situation. For a year and a half she lived with the Tibetans, cooking over open fires and enjoying the simplest of existences. She found the Tibetans open and loving and she got to know them well. She took an interest in their religion but never thought of adopting it for herself.

She was becoming confident within herself and determined not to return to society in the West until she was strong enough to cope with that kind of life.

Her first sign of real strength was when she wrote to Alan breaking up their relationship. He refused to accept this and went to India to make her change her mind. All the usual threats were used but now she could cope with them and was strong enough to stand her ground. Alan left without her.

Then she wrote to her parents asking for their forgiveness for all her behaviour in the past. She saw herself as 'little me' and 'big me'. The 'big me' was her and God. It was then that she was strong and life had meaning. The 'little me' was her on her own, trying to live her own life. She saw her journey at that time as an attempt to keep the balance between the 'little me', that had negative emotions and huge needs, and the 'big me' with a heart that embraces everyone. She is on the same journey today, making a constant choice between the two 'me's every day, every minute, every second, and she would say that she feels herself to be a beginner on that journey.

She returned to England and trained as a Montessori teacher, but it was too soon. She was not ready yet. She still could not cope with life around her and she had no friends. It was back to India and life with the Tibetans again. For ten more months she lived the simple life, with long walks and plenty of time for deep thinking. The next time she returned to England she was ready.

At first nothing happened and she could not see her way ahead, but she started attending St James's Church, Piccadilly, in the heart of London, and though she did not get close to anyone there she was happy in the atmosphere of what is quite an unusual Anglican church. The rector, Donald Reeves, was appointed in 1980 and no one would have been too surprised if he had struggled on with a handful of people for a couple of years and then closed the place down. Instead he drew up a ten-year plan and this is now rapidly coming to fruition. As soon as you step through the door its unorthodoxy challenges you. Your mind fills with questions, but you are slow to voice them because the place is now full of people. You see things you do not expect to find in a Christian place of worship, while some items you would expect to find are missing.

It dawned on me as I walked though the beautiful building, where a lunch-time lecture on 'Justice and Peace' had ended and where busy preparations were being made for an evening orchestral concert, that what I was seeing in Joanna Berry was a microcosm of the life of this church. Joanna was not saying the things I had expected her to say. She expressed ideas that surprised me. Yet the end product was a young girl with a clear faith in God, who had been able to forgive totally the people who had planted the bomb that killed her father. She sees forgiveness as a quality that you choose to accept or reject, but the choosing is a continuous act not a once-only decision. She describes it as a continuous act of surrendering to God.

I am quite certain that she did not pick up all her ideas from St James's. Much of her development took place in the vast expanse of Indian mountains and the shut-away life of Tibetan refugees, but the biggest single factor in making Joanna into a girl with faith and a purpose for living was the death of her father amid all the rubble of a bombed hotel.

So can true forgiveness only be found through the trauma of the most tragic deaths? Joanna Berry and Pearl McKeown (Chapter 1) did not walk along the same paths through life, but the turning point for both was the killing of someone very close to them. Forgiveness for the world came through the death of Christ, and every event of that kind is going to either turn people to God or away from him. There is no escaping from death in this world. It demands some kind of reaction from everyone.

Government business had taken Joanna's father to Africa where he met a missionary who possessed nothing by the world's standards. Her father realized that only a power or a being far greater than the missionary could have drawn someone to live such a life of dedicated service to others under the most primitive conditions. Joanna was able to have a heart-to-heart talk with her father after that, and sensed that he was then understanding what her stay in India was all about. Perhaps the motive for her stay in those mountainous regions was far bigger than she, Sir Anthony or anyone else could comprehend.

Joanna decided that she would go to Africa. There was no particular reason. It just seemed the right step to take. She let her flat, packed her bags and moved in with her sister for a night. She phoned her father, hoping to see him, but as that was not possible she said goodbye to him on the phone. It was their last conversation together.

When the funeral was over Joanna realized she had lost her father, and her flat, and even Africa was now out of the question. She contacted the people who had rented her flat and asked if she could have it back, but they refused. That seemed a cruel decision and added to her sense of devastation. The lease was for six months so there was nothing to do but wait. She set herself a deadline of 1st January by which she would start working somewhere, somehow.

The family went on a skiing holiday that Christmas and it was enjoyable until the last day when her sister was badly injured. They managed to be happy as a family, but each one was nursing her own private grief.

Joanna started working with dying children at Ormond Street Hospital in London. Gone was her dream of saving the world. Now she was getting on with the job in hand, helping a few young suffering lives as best she could.

Several months before her father's death Joanna had met Peter, a young man with a fair beard and cheerful disposi-

31

tion, who had visited the Iona Community on six occasions. During days of meditation he had begun to feel the pain of what was happening to the Irish people. The bombs and bullets were very much a shared experience for him, and when the IRA brought that tragedy to Brighton he and Joanna were able to share their innermost thoughts together.

It was a shock to Joanna on the day she realized that someone had actually wanted to kill her father. Part of her reacted in anger to that thought. The anger shot out in different directions: towards the IRA, at Mrs Thatcher, against God. This was her 'little me' in action. When she resisted this, trying to hold on to her relationship with God (her 'big me'), she thought differently. Her desire was for reconciliation. She would love to have been able to reconcile the whole Northern Ireland conflict within herself. Peter helped her to work this concept out in her life. She resisted taking sides in the conflict. She wanted to think beyond the act of forgiveness because, she reasoned, if you forgive someone that means the person has done something that needs to be forgiven. She had to resolve in her mind whether she was being judgemental by deciding that some acts that people commit are of such a nature that they need forgiveness. Peter walked with her down this road of exploration and helped her to come to right decisions.

She asked God to do three things in her life: to help her continuously, to guide her along the road she was taking, and to bring her into the experience of complete forgiveness.

People tried to draw her into a set area of beliefs that they had drawn up for people in her position, but she resisted this. She wanted God's answer, untainted by what anyone's religion may have formulated.

God's intervention when it came was quite dramatic, although when Joanna talks about it now she leaves out many of the details of that experience because they have lost their importance in comparison with the outcome that is still so vivid to her.

She was travelling home on the last underground train

one night, by herself, when she felt a strong compulsion to leave the train at the next station, even though that was nowhere near home. I have heard Joanna relate this experience and say: 'God told me to get out at the next station.' At other times she has left out the reference to God's voice. Anyone who has heard God speak can be faced with a similar dilemma, because they may not hear a voice. There is no doubt in Joanna's mind that it was not her idea to be alone on a dark night in an unfamiliar part of London with the last train disappearing in the distance.

Walking down that dark street she decided she would stop the first taxi that came and go home. When a taxi appeared she found a man by her side asking to share the taxi with her. That was a tricky situation in itself, but they both got in and talked together in the back seat. The man was from Northern Ireland and said to her: 'Do you know that my brother was shot dead by British soldiers in Northern Ireland?' Her reply was: 'Do you know that my father was killed by an IRA bomb in Brighton?'

They shared their feelings and thoughts together and in doing so were building a bridge that reconciled them to each other. Instead of fermenting anger or resentment they were releasing it and letting it go.

Joanna could see God totally in that meeting. It was her first experience of building a bridge of reconciliation and she knew she had found the one thing she wanted more than anything else. To meet a man who was associated in some way with the IRA and to be able to cope with that meeting was a miracle in her life that took her by surprise.

Her father's death was now taking on a positive aspect she had not been able to see before. If he had to die, the 12th October, 1984 could well have been the right time in God's eyes. Her father was a different man after his visit to Africa. His relationship with her was deeper and more real since their heart-to-heart talk. He had achieved more for peace in the last few years of his life than at any time before. Now she felt ready to go to Ireland to meet the people for herself.

She went to a conference in Northern Ireland at the ancient town of Benburb in Co. Tyrone. About eighty people attended from both sides of the Irish border and Joanna fell in love with them all. The leader of the conference was Elizabeth Kubler-Ross, originally from Switzerland but resident in the USA, who encouraged a sense of trust between the people. There was lots of singing and people stayed up until the early hours of the morning, sharing experiences. Joanna was getting happier with each day, but she noticed that many others were grieving. On the last night of the conference people spoke from their personal experience of the sad things that had happened to them. Joanna was the last to share and she spoke of the coming to terms with the death of her father. It was a positive message that lasted for half an hour and though her obvious happiness seemed to surprise people at first, many said how much they had been helped by what she said.

From Benburb Joanna went to Rostrevor to visit the Christian Renewal Centre where a community of Catholics and Protestants are engaged in a ministry of reconciliation all over the nation. She arrived there on 12th July, the date on which Protestants in Northern Ireland celebrate the Battle of the Boyne of 1690 with parades, beating drums and high-powered political speeches. On that date the community at Rostrevor always hold a public service of reconciliation with a Catholic priest and a Protestant minister sharing the platform. On that occasion the meeting was at the Warrenpoint Town Hall and Joanna spoke to the hundreds of people present, Catholics and Protestants, about the forgiveness that the Lord had enabled her to feel and express. It was the largest meeting at which she had ever spoken. At the end people surrounded her and embraced her.

Back in London Joanna told me that she could see the value in people referring to themselves as 'Christians' in Northern Ireland as it did away with the labels of

'Protestant' and 'Catholic' that caused so much conflict. In England she doubted the value of the label 'Christian' because it had religious connotations for people who were genuinely seeking God but had given up on their concept of religion. In a television programme in England Joanna said that she would not refer to herself as a Christian. That caused many listeners to think that she was saying she is not a Christian. To me it sounded the same as I hear people saying in Northern Ireland: 'I would never let anyone refer to me as a Protestant.' The speakers are not necessarily Roman Catholics or Jews. They simply do not want to use divisive labels.

Joanna's vision is to bring about reconciliation in every sphere possible, and above all to experience that reconciliation in her own life. She has correspondence with a member of the IRA who is in prison. She has had a long talk with a member of Sinn Fein in the Republic of Ireland. In her own words: 'I am left with a burning passion for reconciliation in Northern Ireland. I feel very close to all the Irish now and feel as an English woman that the English have much to learn from them. Maybe we could ask the Irish to forgive us for all we have done and do.'

At the time I interviewed Joanna she was working in a bookshop at St James's Church. Peter was still very much a part of her life. She sees herself as constantly changing. Realizing that she cannot spend the rest of her life talking about her father's death, she is waiting to see what fresh opportunities life will bring to her.

Joanna sees her life at present as a triangle. God is at the apex and she and Peter occupy the other two corners. Together they put God first in everything and at the horizontal level they are in touch to help each other. Through a very hard and difficult road she can now talk from deep experience of what is meant by reconciliation and forgiveness.

3

My Father Is Dead, But ...

In this chapter I am moving away from what I had originally planned. A young man in his early twenties has persuaded me to change my mind.

In planning this book I decided that I would not publish anyone's story unless I could give their correct name and so identify the person clearly. The only exception I was prepared to make was when writing of people I met who are not able to forgive.

Then I met this young man who told me his story and in so doing pleaded for anonymity for the sake of his family. I realize that as he speaks at public meetings and tells his story he is gradually losing that anonymity and one day it may go completely, but that time has not yet come. Violence is a very sensitive issue in Northern Ireland and can have terrifying repercussions on the families of people who speak out about it. I am therefore persuaded that this man's family, still living in Northern Ireland, should have their anonymity respected for as long as that proves possible.

Picture him, therefore, although nameless, a clean shaven, thinly-built young man, relaxing in a chair, a ready smile on his lips but a serious look in his eyes, as though they had seen more than their share of difficult sights in the first quarter of a life. We are sitting in the reception room of a religious order in the Republic of Ireland, a vast building that once housed a hundred students but is now struggling to keep open with sixteen students occupying just one wing of the building.

I ply him with questions and the story unfolds spasmodically, as his memory jumps from one incident to another. I hold him to when he was fifteen years of age, living in Northern Ireland, and to 12th October, 1977, because every second of that day is etched clearly in his mind.

His father was unemployed but was available as a relief bus driver whenever required. One day the father received a phone call asking him to take over a bus the next day in place of a driver on leave. As he was unfamiliar with the route he went out with another man on the day of the phone call and they covered the route together. The next morning he left the house at 6.50 a.m. to be ready to do the first bus run of the day at 7.45 a.m.

He was sitting in the driver's seat waiting for the time to move off. His only concern was that he would be able to remember the route he was to travel. A little girl got on the bus and ran to a back seat. He asked her if she would sit nearer the front as he was unsure of the way and she would be able to help him. The girl asked him not to start just yet as she had two friends who always caught that bus and they had not yet arrived. Then the girl ran to the back again. The driver sat at the wheel waiting. Suddenly the girl heard a loud bang. She saw the driver slump over the wheel and heard him muttering: 'Jesus, Mary and Joseph, have mercy on my soul.'

The driver's son has since talked with that girl and has heard the account from her own lips. She described how two men got on to the bus and started shooting bullets into the driver. Later the surgeons found twenty-eight bullet wounds. The coroner at the inquest said he believed that it would have been the first bullet that killed the driver.

The two men ran away leaving a terrified girl and a dead

man in the bus. So ended another act of violence in Northern Ireland, but there was a different aspect to this one. For one thing that particular area of Northern Ireland had never known a death from terrorist action until that moment, and there has not been another one since. Most tragic of all was the fact that the gunmen had killed the wrong man. They were gunning for the regular driver who had not taken an extra day off in fourteen years and was considered an enemy by the IRA because he served part time with the Ulster Defence Regiment, a volunteer force of part time soldiers. The gunmen did not realize that they were pumping their bullets into the body of a man against whom they had no grudge at all. It was a tragic case of mistaken identity.

A priest took on the sorry task of going to a local school to break the news to the dead man's son. The youngster listened, hardly able to take in what he was hearing, stunned to silence and in a state of shock. He went home to be with his mother, knowing she would be grief-stricken and wondering how he, at fifteen years the eldest member of the family, could cope with such a responsibility.

A friend had called at his home to console his mother, only to find on her arrival that the mother had not yet heard the news, so the friend had to break it to her.

Although dazed by what had happened the young teenager found himself having to act as the head of the house, taking decisions and accepting responsibilities that were heavy for such unexperienced shoulders. There was the press to deal with too. Radio, television and the papers were crowding round the door of the house, wanting to get in, to take pictures, to ask questions. The family drew up a prepared statement and issued it with some photographs of the dead man, and in so doing managed to keep the press outside the door.

Then there was the decision about where he should be buried. He was very fond of Donegal and had a summer house there. Someone had to decide and the teenager realized it must be him so he declared that the burial would be in the home town, not Donegal, and that the family would continue living there.

The funeral service was an unreal experience for that young boy. He lived through it in a daze, not feeling anything very much, as though a protective shield had gone up around him. He watched the service on television news that evening and could hardly believe that he had been present at the ceremony and that the coffin he saw on the small screen contained the body of his father.

The weeks that followed were very difficult ones. His mother was so upset that it was not possible to talk with her about how he felt. If anyone mentioned her husband's name in her presence she would burst into tears. There was no one in whom he could confide, but he began his own investigations into what had happened. He talked with the little girl on the bus. He discovered everything he could about that dreadful day, but it was the police who unearthed the full horror of the tragedy. When they had traced the two men and arrested them, the youngster realized that he knew the families concerned. His father had sung for one of the killers at a party the previous week.

Everyone realized that a terrible mistake had been made. No one would have wanted to harm that man. But that does not soften the blow. In some ways it adds salt to the wound. Murder can never be excused by talking about mistaken identity. The man for whom the bullets were intended was also an innocent person and his death would have been just as great a tragedy. These are difficult concepts to grapple with when it is your father who has been murdered.

The guilty men were sentenced to life imprisonment, which in Northern Ireland can mean about eleven years if there is time off for good behaviour. Nine of those eleven years had gone when I spoke to the young man. He is keeping count because he knows that when they come out he will very likely meet them. He has already met some sisters of the killers and talked with them. Perhaps it seems strange to an onlooker, but they talked about everything except the killing or the father who was dead. After all, what could anyone say? Both parties would know that any reference to the shooting would sound shallow and meaningless. It was best to keep off the subject. The fact that they were talking together was significant enough in itself.

The next thing I wanted to discover from this young man as we sat together was how he could enter a religious order, be ordained into the priesthood and spend the rest of his life proclaiming the good news of the gospel in Northern Ireland while this terrible tragedy in his family was burning in his soul.

He had felt bitter about what had happened and also that he would never be able to trust anyone again. That was not the best equipping for the priesthood and he knew this, but he didn't seem able to do anything about it. The unforgiving spirit in his heart was going to be a barrier to the outworking of his whole Christian life, but there was no one in whom he could confide and there was no way in which he could change how he felt. The only thing he could accept in his mind was that the two men had ruined one life in his family and he saw no reason why he should allow them to ruin his life as well. His bitterness was hurting no one except himself, but he knew of no surgeon who could operate to remove bitterness.

Then he went to a camp for young people held in Co. Clare. It was a Christian camp called 'Camp with the Lord'. The people who ran it did not make claim to be either Catholic or Protestant. They simply called themselves Christians. There was lots of fun at the camp as well as times for worship, teaching from the Scriptures and prayer. He especially valued the opportunity to spend time in prayer. He really wanted that bitterness to go and the barrier to be removed. It was that for which he was praying.

One of the leaders, a man from Dublin, was the kind of person you could get alongside and share your problems with. This man prayed with him. It was a very specific prayer and one that God answered in a remarkable way. It was as though the Holy Spirit brought the peace of Christ into his life. The bitterness that had begun to really hurt him left. It was a complete deliverance. For the first time since his father's death he cried, and the release of tears brought a new freedom to his life. For the first time he could talk about his father freely and openly.

Now he felt free to serve God and in so doing to use his own experience to describe the message of forgiveness as a reality and not just a theory written about in books.

The desire to serve the Lord full time had come just a few days before his father's death. A mission was being held in his local church at home and in the course of it the priests re-enacted the Last Supper as a dramatic presentation. His father was sitting near the front of the church and was called on to assist in the presentation of the foot-washing ceremony. Watching his father and others act this out gave the young man a desire to present the gospel in equally memorable ways. He decided to join an order that would provide opportunities for such service.

At the age of seventeen he knew in his own heart what he wanted to do, but the advice he was receiving was that he should become a diocesan priest and work in a parish rather than join an order. He did not feel he could stand against his superiors, so he set off for Maynooth, in Co. Kildare, to be trained as a priest. It was a mistake from the moment he set foot in the place, but he stuck it out for three years. He was never happy there and could not accept the people or the environment. He embibed philosophy for three years and then left.

He had no plans except for a deep desire to help people with their problems. He found a man with a similar vision who had set up a tiny office with one girl to help him in voluntary social work. They teamed up and having divided the office into half they got involved with the unemployed, unmarried mothers, the handicapped, people trying to cope with a death in the family and the large number of people in need who knew nothing about the benefits to which they were entitled. It was all done on a voluntary basis and the work rapidly expanded, moving to larger offices and reaching many cities and rural areas. They even tried to arouse some interest in the problems of the Third World, but that venture fell through.

He was there for two years and he enjoyed every minute of it. It was a great time of learning, gaining experience and perhaps, most important of all, being able to show compassion and care for people in their need.

Then he moved into the religious order in which he had first been interested. It was there that we met one evening after he had finished his lectures for the day. He has still a long way to go in his training, but the order encourages students to engage in practical work so he is out and about proclaiming the gospel in ways aimed to attract the attention of young people who have given up on the church. He had just returned from conducting a retreat in a comprehensive school where he found that many of the older students did not believe in God and would say: 'The church does not represent us.' He told them about his father, of the miracle that happened in his own life and of how he was now able to forgive totally the man who did the killing. The first reaction was one of total silence. The questions came later and many of the young people obviously found it hard to believe that it was possible to receive such a gift of forgiveness.

He has no hesitation in describing his experience as a miracle. There is no way in which he, humanly speaking, could forgive the men who killed his father. Even today he finds he needs to read the Scriptures each morning so as to lay the foundations of forgiveness in his life afresh. 'If I dropped the word of God I would lose the ability to forgive.'

Next I talked to him about the day when he will meet the two men who killed his father. He knows the day of their release from prison is drawing near and that he is certain to

42

meet them. He has thought about that meeting and he explained first his reaction to the men as individuals. He believes that the words Christ spoke from the cross apply to them in that they did not know what they were doing. He also realizes that their lives may have been threatened. They would have been acting under authority from the IRA hierarchy and if they had refused to do the killing, revenge might have been taken on them. The use of intimidation is a strong weapon among the people of violence in Northern Ireland and the residents of that province know only too well how it operates.

When the meeting with the two men takes place, there are three questions he wants to put to them. He will be listening to their answers very carefully. The first is: Why did they do it? Then: How did they feel when they realized who it was they had killed? Finally: How do they feel now?

Perhaps the last question is the most important, revealing as it will what has been going on in their lives during their years of imprisonment. I asked the question: 'Will you tell them that you forgive them?' He thought that one through and said: 'I do not think it should be necessary to say that to them. I would hope that my attitude towards them in meeting and talking with them will show that I have no bitterness or resentment towards them.'

The experience of receiving the gift of forgiveness has clearly revolutionized this man's ministry, and when his training is completed I can see him influencing countless lives throughout Ireland. He wants to work particularly in Northern Ireland, as that is where he believes his message most needs to be heard. Whoever sits under his preaching is almost certain to hear three themes coming through very clearly. Each will have its own peculiar impact and together they make up a powerful message.

He will dwell on the full implications of chapter 13 in 1 Corinthians. It is his favourite Bible passage, full of what the love of God is like and what it can accomplish in anyone's life. You can imagine him getting to grips with such phrases as: '[Love] is not easily angered, it keeps no record of wrongs' (verse 5). Then he will begin a meditation on the cross, that mighty demonstration of God's love, and when he gets to the words: 'Father, forgive them for they know not what they do,' he will slip into his testimony, telling his own experience of the gift of forgiveness. The power of this message is already evident in his ministry whenever he reaches out to the people around the college.

The week in which we met he had invited a group of young people to meet with him once a week for a discussion evening. There was an immediate response though he limited the number to twenty-five so that everyone would take part and not get lost in a crowd. He stipulates that each of their views must be respected no matter how stupid they might seem. Everyone must be listened to as they deal with such subjects as 'Who am I?'; 'The good qualities of Jesus Christ' and 'Where am I going?' At the end of the series they will devise their own liturgy for a Mass and invite their parents and friends to attend. By that time they will all know about love, the cross and forgiveness.

He can remember the time when the Mass was for Catholics and the Bible was for Protestants and the two never seemed to meet. He is now rectifying that, using the Mass as a means of proclaiming the word. His main preparation for the full-time ministry that lies before him is that of prayer. His order has five sessions of prayer a day, and in addition he has his own prayer time. He finds that the people he meets in the Republic are not interested in what is happening in the North. They do not see it as being any part of their problem. For him it is different. He is a Northerner. Two of the people who are studying with him have had relations killed through terrorist action. With those two men around him he has not escaped from the problem by going south, but he is not looking for an escape, he wants to be involved in the problem. He is looking forward to returning to the North. He will not in any way be a political person there, as he has no leanings to any one party, but he knows he has found a teaching and an experience that the people in the North need to know about.

Before we parted I asked him to summarize the change that has taken place in his life. He smiled and said: 'I used to say, "My father is dead. I do not have a father." Now I can say, "My father is dead. Through his death I have grown spiritually and as a person. I have more understanding and compassion."'

That is his **miracle** of forgiveness.

4

A Biblical Perspective

In this chapter I will go right through the Bible from Genesis to Revelation picking up the thread of forgiveness that is to be found in almost every book. In this way we will start off with a right perspective of what the Bible as a whole teaches on the subject. Our understanding of any subject should never be based on one or two texts. Only the whole word of God can reveal the complete truth of what God is saying. Obviously there has to be a process of selection, but we will try to treat the Bible fairly and to let the whole book speak as God's revelation to us on forgiveness.

There is a very beautiful example of forgiveness in Genesis that covers many important aspects of what the Bible as a whole has to say on the subject. This is the account of Joseph's brothers coming to receive his forgiveness for the dreadful way they had treated him in selling him as a slave and then telling his father he was dead (Genesis 50:15–21).

Listen to their request: 'I ask you to forgive your brothers the sins and the wrongs they committed in treating you so badly' (verse 17).

Notice their use of the term 'brothers'. A sin of the kind they committed against their brother Joseph breaks the family relationship. Brothers can no longer have fellowship together once one sins against the other. There is nothing

46

that causes division quicker than sin. Sin is always divisive whether in a family, a church or a nation, and it is especially so in our relationship with God.

Sin does not stop brothers from being brothers, any more than sin can stop God being our Father, but the fellowship is broken. There is no sense of belonging. Communication stops and a great barrier is erected between the one who sins and the one who is sinned against.

When seeking forgiveness it is important to ask for a restoration of that relationship. We need to call God 'Father' again, quite deliberately. We need to look at the one we have wronged and call him what he truly is, 'brother'. Let it be seen that we are looking for more than forgiveness on its own. We want to feel the family relationship again. Being a brother again should be as important to us as knowing that we are forgiven.

This is illustrated in the New Testament when Saul becomes a Christian and Ananias goes to visit him (Acts 9). Saul had spent years persecuting the church and throwing Christians into prison. Now he embraces the Christian faith and has to understand that every Christian is his brother or sister, that he is in the family of which God is the Father. He is about to meet his first Christian brother.

Ananias walks into the house where Saul is staying and says: 'Brother Saul' (verse 17). That was an act of forgiveness. Ananias was speaking for all his fellow-Christians and saying, 'Saul, we forgive you and therefore we rejoice to receive you as our brother.' When you show or accept forgiveness, a relationship is restored. If the relationship is not put right, then the forgiveness is incomplete.

Returning to Joseph and his brothers, the next thing to notice is that 'Joseph wept' (verse 17). That is the experience of forgiveness. True forgiveness can never be cold, hard and matter-of-fact. It can never be legal—you have confessed so I will forgive because that is what the Bible says I should do. That is not real enough, genuine enough. Sin is painful. Forgiveness is joyful. Between the act of sinning and the fact of forgiveness there is a price to be paid. There is the cost of humility, seeking forgiveness, reaching out to the one hurt. The relief when that takes place is so real that it is expressed in tears, laughter or some other emotional reaction. The person who forgives also pays a price. The willingness to put away the hurt, the anger, the resentment, or whatever effect the sin had, brings a great relief that can often be expressed only in tears.

Christ wept over the people of Jerusalem (Luke 19:41), but they were tears of sorrow because no one was seeking forgiveness or repenting of their sins. The tears that come with the experience of being forgiven or of forgiving someone are a strange mixture of joy, relief and deep healing.

The moment of forgiveness is a very humble one. The slightest trace of pride in the heart will prevent the forgiveness from being fulfilled. The brothers of Joseph 'Threw themselves down before him. "We are your slaves", they said' (verse 18).

Lying prostrate on the ground is a lowly place to be. The sinner seeking forgiveness does not stand before the throne of God. His place is to follow his heart to the lowliest position. When you walk up to your brother to seek forgiveness you do not slap him on the back with a broad grin on your face. You come in the spirit of humility, willing to take the lowliest place in his presence.

Joseph's response is a perfect model for us all. He asked: 'Am I in the place of God?' (verse 19). Only God has the right to judge a person for wrongdoing. We must never play at being God when someone comes to us seeking forgiveness. The other person may have wronged us, but we have committed more sins than we could count so we are in no position to judge or condemn.

Finally, we note that the person who forgives does not leave it at that. The act of forgiving is not the end of the matter. There is a continuing ministry that is needed. Joseph said: 'I will provide for you and your children' (verse 21). Reconciliation between two people who have become separated by sin is not just a matter of words, but rather of a growing together, a mutual concern for each other and a willingness to minister to each others' needs.

In the book of Exodus there is an important principle to be learned. When a sin is committed and forgiveness is sought there must be a willingness to cease committing that sin. If the forgiveness that is offered does not result in the giving up of the sin then the forgiveness has not been received properly.

This can be seen in the example of Pharaoh who said to Moses: 'Now forgive my sin *once more* and pray to the Lord your God to take this deadly plague away from me' (Exodus 10:17). The 'once more' denotes that Pharaoh was continuing with the same sin, and seeking forgiveness every time he committed it. The sin and the forgiveness were continuing on parallel lines but never getting to grips with each other. True forgiveness fully received will result in the giving up of the sin.

One way in which this can fail to operate is when the person seeking forgiveness does not forgive himself for what he has done. As I am forgiven so I must at the same time forgive myself and not go round with a guilty conscience. Forgiveness cleanses. We must receive the cleansing as well as the pardon.

Pharaoh referred to the Lord as the God of Moses, but not as his own God—'Pray to the Lord *your God*.' Pharaoh felt no compulsion to obey someone else's God. It is only as we accept God as the Lord of our lives that we will begin to obey his injunction at the time of forgiveness: 'Go now and leave your life of sin' (John 8:11).

In Exodus 32 we learn an important lesson on the role of the intercessor in the realm of forgiveness. The people of Israel had sinned against God and one righteous person in their midst decides to intervene on their behalf. Moses prays: 'But now, please forgive their sin—but if not, then blot me out of the book you have written' (verse 32). This one-sentence prayer may be held up as a perfect example of how to intercede on behalf of other people who are living in a situation of sin and disobedience to God. Sin comes between a people and their God, so Moses stands in that gap seeking to bring about reconciliation through the ministry of forgiveness. There is more to this than praying for the people or than asking God to be merciful to the people. Moses, who had remained faithful to God, showed his willingness to take the people's sins upon himself and to be punished for them.

The supreme example of this is Christ who was able to pray from the cross: 'Father, forgive them.' He was sinless and need never have died but he took the sin of the world upon himself, and that separated him from his Father and brought death to his whole being.

The intercessor stands in the gap between a sinful nation or individual and a holy God. He so pleads for forgiveness that he is prepared to be counted guilty of the sin which makes the prayer necessary. Peter got it right when he wrote: 'He himself bore our sins in his body on the tree' (1 Peter 2:24). It was *our* sins on *his* body that turned his death into the greatest act of intercession.

We meet Moses the intercessor again in the book of Numbers. Look at his prayer there: 'In accordance with your great love, forgive the sin of these people, just as you have pardoned them from the time they left Egypt until now' (14:19). He is again asking God to forgive the people but this time his request is based on God's great love. True forgiveness always stems from great love. A shallow love may result in the words of forgiveness being spoken but the act of forgiveness never taking place. Moses was on sure ground when he reminded God of his great love. We need to base our prayer for forgiveness on the knowledge of the same love.

'This is love: not that we loved God, but that he loved us and sent his Son as an atoning sacrifice for our sins' (1 John 4:10). If ever you doubt God's willingness to forgive the sin of anyone, remind yourself of the Lord's great love.

In the book of Deuteronomy we find a completely different aspect of forgiveness—the possibility that in some cases the Lord might not be willing to forgive. It was Moses who came to the conclusion that an instance could arise when God would not be willing to grant forgiveness: 'The Lord will never be willing to forgive him; his wrath and zeal will burn against that man' (29:20).

This is not an isolated instance in Scripture. Joshua came to the same conclusion when he stated: 'He will not forgive your rebellion and your sins' (Joshua 24:19). God's unwillingness to forgive is stated as a fact in 2 Kings 24:4, 'The Lord was not willing to forgive.'

In the first case Moses is thinking of the person who decides to live anyway he likes, to ignore any commandments that do not suit him and yet still expect to benefit from God's blessings of health, food and protection. Such a person sees no need to repent for the way he lives and is not seeking God's forgiveness for the sins he commits. If forgiveness is not sought the heart of God does not move out to forgive. The father moves out to meet the prodigal son as soon as the son decides to move back towards the father. It is equally true that the father made no move towards the son until the son decided to leave his life of rebellion. God is always willing to forgive, but will wait for the rebellious sinner to start seeking forgiveness.

Since the day of Pentecost there are many evidences of the Spirit taking the initiative and reaching out to the rebellious sinner to convict him of his need of forgiveness. It is always important when studying an Old Testament teaching to ask two questions: What difference has the cross made to this teaching and what difference has Pentecost made to this teaching?

In the case of Joshua's statement that the Lord would not forgive, the people accepted that almost as a challenge and responded to it in the right way. They promised to obey the Lord and to serve him and it was then up to Joshua to lay down for them the kind of obedience and service that the

Lord required of the people.

In the passage in 2 Kings the Lord had come in judgement on the people for their rebellion, and there could not be any forgiveness until that period of judgement had been fulfilled. The cross has made a great difference to that teaching. The judgement of God fell upon Jesus at the cross when he bore the sin of the whole world. Today we are under grace and not under judgement. This is the day when all may find forgiveness. But when the time of grace ends then the judgement of God will fall on all who did not avail themselves of God's grace and mercy.

Samuel takes us a stage further by showing that forgiveness is not to be given lightly. King Saul asked for forgiveness from Samuel and also for help in getting back into a right relationship with God, but Samuel knew that God had already rejected Saul as king and was putting someone else on the throne in his place. He therefore knew that full reconciliation in the way that Saul wanted was no longer possible.

The conversation between the two men went like this:

> Saul said to Samuel, 'I have sinned. I violated the Lord's command and your instructions. I was afraid of the people and so I gave in to them. Now I beg you, forgive my sin and come back with me, so that I may worship the Lord.' But Samuel said to him, 'I will not go back with you. You have rejected the word of the Lord, and the Lord has rejected you as king over Israel!' (1 Samuel 15:24–26).

As the story continues it is seen that a reconciliation does take place between Saul and the Lord, but only on the Lord's terms. The Lord insisted that David be anointed as future king in Saul's place. Samuel had to be careful that he did not go further than God was prepared to go. Samuel might easily have been big-hearted and assured Saul that God would forgive him and cause his reign to prosper. Instead he had to know the will of the Lord and to discern

Saul's future role. Forgiveness and reconciliation are always possible to the repentant sinner, but God will be just in deciding what our future role will be in his service. If we are unfaithful in small things we can expect forgiveness, but must not presume that the Lord will then entrust us with big responsibilities.

Judgement must always be left in the hands of God. It is never for us to judge or to seek revenge. We are in the ministry of forgiveness and reconciliation. God alone is Judge. David set out to get revenge for what Nabal had done to him and his men. On his way he met Nabal's wife, Abigail, coming to intercede on behalf of her husband. She was seeking mercy, forgiveness and reconciliation on behalf of Nabal. 'Please forgive your servant's offence, for the Lord will certainly make a lasting dynasty for my master, because he fights the Lord's battles. Let no wrongdoing be found in you as long as you live' (1 Samuel 25:28). That last sentence shows that Abigail realized that David could be doing wrong by taking the law into his own hands and seeking revenge.

David wisely heeded what Abigail said and left judgement to the Lord. The Lord acted as judge according to Old Testament principles—'About ten days later, the Lord struck Nabal and he died' (verse 38). If David had killed Nabal he would have been acting as God. The cross makes a tremendous difference to the way in which the Lord waits in mercy and grace before pronouncing judgement on any-one, but the principle remains: 'Moreover, the Father judges no-one, but has entrusted all judgement to the Son' (John 5:22). If even the Father stands back so as to ensure that Christ alone is the Judge, what right have we to act as judge, or to seek revenge, on any person?

The dedication of Solomon's temple in Jerusalem, as recorded in 1 Kings, presents many facets of forgiveness. If we see this Old Testament place of worship as a picture of the church today, with the cross standing resolutely between the two, then some important aspects of forgiveness emerge.

Solomon saw the temple as a place of forgiveness. 'Hear the supplication of your servant and of your people Israel when they pray towards this place. Hear from heaven, your dwelling-place, and when you hear, forgive' (1 Kings 8:30). Any coming together of God's people should always constitute a setting where forgiveness operates.

Solomon's next prayer was: 'Hear from heaven and forgive the sin of your people Israel and bring them back to the land you gave to their fathers' (verse 34). Solomon could see that a forgiven people should be back in that place where they could receive all the blessings God had stored up for them as their inheritance. The Christian who disobeys God and then repents and receives his forgiveness is able to experience God's blessings pouring back into his life. Solomon seemed to sense the importance of getting back to the place where God's blessings rest.

Then Solomon becomes very practical: 'Hear from heaven and forgive the sin of your servants, your people Israel. Teach them the right way to live' (verse 36). The receiving of forgiveness must be accompanied by a changed way of living. Sin is an act of disobedience. Forgiveness must bear the fruit of obedience. That was so clear to Solomon. It is part of the thread of truth running through the whole of this teaching.

But Solomon is still praying: 'Forgive and act' (verse 39). If I am to allow God to forgive me then I must be prepared for God to act in every other way he may want to in my life. God does not simply forgive and then move on to someone else's problem. He continues to act in our lives to enable us not to sin in that way again. 'Forgive and act' is a great injunction. In legal terms an injunction is a process that either causes a person to do something or, more usually, causes them to refrain from doing something. That is how God acts.

Solomon's final request was a wonderfully all-embracing plea: 'Forgive your people, who have sinned against you; forgive all the offences they have committed against you' (verse 50). Notice that little word 'all'. The forgiveness we need is not only for one or two specific sins that we confess, but for the very fact that we are sinners. The whole factor of sin in our natures and personalities needs dealing with through the healing of forgiveness. Just as love is all-embracing so forgiveness must never exclude any aspect of sin in a person's life. We can never say: 'I forgive you of this but I cannot forgive you of that.' Solomon has it right. Cleansing is needed from 'all the offences'.

To conclude this scene at the dedication of the temple, turn to the Lord and hear what he has to say. When the temple had been dedicated God spoke: 'If my people, who are called by my name, will humble themselves and pray and seek my face and turn from their wicked ways, then will I hear from heaven and will forgive their sin and will heal their land' (2 Chronicles 7:14). That was the answer to prayer that Solomon needed to hear. That promise is the proof that Solomon was praying along the right lines. Those are still the implications of forgiveness for today.

Now look at the example of Naaman, the man cured of leprosy by God. He knew he would have to return to the pagan king for whom he worked. That king would expect Naaman to accompany him when he went to worship in a pagan temple. Worse than that, the king would be leaning on Naaman's arm and when the king bowed before the idol Naaman would have to bow with him. That was a compromising situation to be in. Listen to Naaman's prayer:

'May the Lord forgive your servant for this one thing: When my master enters the temple of Rimmon to bow down and he is leaning on my arm and I bow there also—when I bow down in the temple of Rimmon, may the Lord forgive your servant for this' (2 Kings 5:18).

How do you react to that prayer? I think it is an excellent one that fits into many difficult situations in life. The test, however, is not our reaction but how did Elisha, the man used by God to heal Naaman, react? He listened to that prayer of Naaman and said: 'Go in peace' (verse 19). It was a good prayer in the eyes of Elisha. To judge the rightness of that prayer it is necessary to have a correct concept of the greatness of God in his magnanimity. God is much more generous in his understanding and forgiveness than we are often willing to accept. Be honest with God about your circumstances at home, in the office, with friends or wherever problems arise. Ask him to understand and forgive. Then 'go in peace'.

The book of Job makes an important distinction between the times when God judges sin and the times when God tests faith. Thanks to the negative thinking of friends who failed to discern correctly what was happening in Job's life, he began to think that it must be because of sin in his life that so much misfortune was happening to him. The trouble was that when he began confessing every conceivable sin to the Lord his circumstances did not improve. Trouble still continued to pile on top of trouble. So he asked some pretty direct questions to God: 'Why do you not pardon my offences and forgive my sins? For I shall soon lie down in the dust; you will search for me, but I shall be no more' (Job 7:21).

Job had reached the end of his tether. If things did not improve soon he felt as though he would die. Job had been listening to the wrong people. He should have been listening to the Lord who said of Job: 'He is blameless and upright, a man who fears God and shuns evil' (Job 1:8). Sin was not Job's problem. Job was being tried because he was righteous and not because he was sinful. God does not put sinners to the test. It is the good, righteous people who are burned alive at the stake, thrown to the lions in a Roman arena, locked away in solitary confinement, banished to a labour camp in Siberia. God knows their faith will never waver. He can depend on them and that is why they are chosen.

Job's prayer should not have been for forgiveness but rather for strength to stand firm in his faith, and to thank

56

God for the privilege of being chosen to prove to the world the reality of faith. We are all prone to listen to the wrong people and forget that the devil is the father of lies and a deceiver. We need to see ourselves in times of suffering through the eyes of Jesus. He sees his people as a forgiven people. It was Job who triumphed in the end and his friends who had to seek forgiveness.

The book of Psalms has a lot to teach on the subject of forgiveness but there are two significant lessons that have not been dealt with so far. The first deals with the sins we may have committed but of which we are not conscious. Listen to the psalmist David: 'Who can discern his errors? Forgive my hidden faults' (Psalm 19:22). David asked God to forgive the sins in his life that were hidden to him and of which he was not conscious. That is a good prayer that God will always honour, and in his time he may reveal those sins to us. In the meantime we can know that even they are covered by Christ's death on the cross.

The second lesson concerns the motive for which we seek forgiveness. Hear David praying again: 'For the sake of your name, O Lord, forgive my iniquity, though it is great' (Psalm 25:11). David was more concerned about the reputation of the Lord's name than about what people might say about himself. He realized that when he, a man of God, sinned it was the Lord's name that suffered. His prayer for forgiveness was not for his own sake but for the sake of the Lord's name.

The same concern to honour the name of the Lord is found in Psalm 79, even though it was not written by David: 'Help us, O God our Saviour, for the glory of your name; deliver us and atone for our sins for your name's sake' (verse 9). David's prayer was for his own sin, but this one is for the sin of the people as a whole. In each case, however, the motive for seeking forgiveness is so that the name of the Lord will be honoured. This is the right motive for every prayer for forgiveness. It is much more important that the Lord's name should be preserved than that my character should be protected.

Now let us look at forgiveness from yet another light. This time we are in the book of Jeremiah. Never under-estimate the influence that one forgiven sinner, who has become righteous in the eyes of God, can have on a community or even a whole city. For the sake of ten righteous people God would have spared the whole city of Sodom. If ten such people had existed in that town they would very likely have thought that their lives were making no impact at all. What could ten people do in the face of a whole city? They could have saved the city from destruction if they had been there. God would have taken notice of even ten and would have spared the rest.

Perhaps the number is even lower than ten and you are the only Christian in your situation. What influence can you possibly have? Let God answer that question: 'If you can find but one person who deals honestly and seeks the truth, I will forgive this city' (Jeremiah 5:1). The city was Jerusalem and God needed only one righteous person there for the whole population to be saved. This shows how important it is for one person to seek forgiveness, cleansing and holiness so that they can stand righteous in any situation and see the salvation of the Lord at work. It is not just for your sake that you need forgiveness, or for the sake of the Lord's name, but also for the sake of the people with whom you live or work.

The influence of the church, with all its weakness, in the world today is such that the judgement of God will not fall so long as the church is here. When the church is removed then judgement will come, but today the church is the salvation of the world.

Jeremiah suffered terribly for his righteousness. Nearly everyone rejected his message. Eventually he had a quiet word with the Lord about the people who opposed him: 'Do not forgive their crimes or blot out their sins from your sight. Let them be overthrown before you; deal with them in the time of your anger' (18:23). Notice that Jeremiah was

58

not taking the law into his own hands and avenging the people. He was leaving judgement to the Lord and just dropping a few hints as to how it might be carried out. It is all right to pray like this provided you really are leaving the outcome to the Lord, and not trying to be judge and executioner yourself. God was fully able to be Judge on that occasion: 'I am going to bring disaster on this place that will make the ears of everyone who hears of it tingle' (19:3). This adds further substance to the lesson already learned that God alone is Judge in every situation and we must never try to avenge those who oppose us.

Jeremiah also underlines the fact that forgiveness and cleansing must always go together. Forgiveness that still leaves the stain of sin on your heart or mind is not true forgiveness. 'I will cleanse them from all the sins they have committed against me and will forgive all their sin of rebellion against me' (33:8). Since the cross, cleansing comes through the shed blood of Christ, but even in the Old Testament the promise of cleansing was there. The knowledge of God's forgiveness coupled with the experience of cleansing lifts the whole burden of sin from us and sets us free from its clutches.

The message of the gospel carries two emphases—the danger of hell and the promise of heaven. Together they provide a good balance to the message. Even when only one emphasis is preached it can still draw a response from the listener. People have sought forgiveness out of fear of hell, while others have come through preaching on God's love. God recognized this when he said: 'Perhaps when the people of Judah hear about every disaster I plan to inflict on them, each of them will turn from his wicked way; then I will forgive their wickedness and their sin' (36:3). The Lord recognized that the message of judgement to come, even without any reference to the mercy of God, could result in people repenting and seeking forgiveness. The person drawn to God by the message of his love may be a warmer-hearted and more compassionate Christian than the one drawn by the fear of judgement to come, but each equally will know the reality of forgiveness.

A point that is completely lost by many Christian people is that when a person is forgiven and cleansed from sin, not a trace of sin is left in his life. The slate is wiped clean. He has become as white as snow or as white as wool. Yet many people appear to be much more conscious of sin in their lives than they are of God's forgiveness and cleansing. Hear the Lord on this subject:

> 'In those days, at that time,' declares the Lord, 'search will be made for Israel's guilt, but there will be none, and for the sins of Judah, but none will be found, for I will forgive the remnant I spare' (Jeremiah 50:20).

Go to a sinner when he has received forgiveness in his life and search for some evidence of sin there and you will not find any. That statement by the Lord in Jeremiah is not easily accepted by Christian people. They will argue against it to try and show that it does not mean what it says. They will argue against the experience of Daniel—'They could find no corruption in him, because he was trustworthy and neither corrupt nor negligent' (Daniel 6:4).

God's forgiveness is not a once-only act. It is a continuous experience. Forgiveness and cleansing are continually applied to the life of the Christian. You may see the outward evidence of sin as a Christian becomes irritable, hot tempered or resentful, but search the heart for the evidence of that sin and you will not find it. The sin is covered by the blood of Jesus. It is washed away—unless the Christian decides to hold on to it and to deny the efficacy of the blood. When Christ returns for his bride, the church, she will be without spot, stain or wrinkle. Search for sin and you will not find it. Somehow a guilt-riddled church has got to get hold of the truth.

Now listen to a heart-rending cry for forgiveness: 'O Lord, listen! O Lord, forgive! O Lord, hear and act! For your sake, O my God, do not delay, because your city and your people bear your Name' (Daniel 9:19). Daniel was praying for God's people, the believers of his day, and was deeply distressed at their lack of faith, failure to reverence the Lord and indifference to the state of the temple. This brings us to the kind of heartfelt prayer that is needed for the state of the Christian church today. There are many Christians who are deeply concerned for the lack of faith within the church, for the absences of real reverence for the Lord and the lack of commitment to him.

The strength of the church lies in its visible unity. Wherever that is lacking then the church appears weak and the world believes it can safely ignore those many church buildings and all that goes on within them. This is why Christ prayed in his last great intercessory prayer on earth: 'May they be brought to complete unity to let the world know that you sent me and have loved them even as you have loved me' (John 17:23). The reason for Christ desiring oneness within the church was not for the sake of the people in the church, but so that the world would come to believe in him. The church will never win the world to Christ until it is seen by the world to be united.

Christians are all one in Christ Jesus. The unity has been brought about by the Holy Spirit who abides within the lives of all Christian people, but the church has decided to speak a lie to the world and to give the impression that we are all divided. All that the world can see is our divisions. We demonstrate it every Sunday in every town and city when the Christian population moves out of their homes on to the streets at around the same time in the morning, but then all head in different directions and enter separate buildings so as to give a clear witness of disunity to the world.

With this realization before us we need to pray as Daniel prayed. He took the line that the Israelites bore God's name, they were known as the people of God, and therefore their disobedience to the Lord was bringing dishonour to God. He was pleading with the Lord to restore his people to obedience, not for their sake, but for the sake of bringing honour to his name. The situation is just the same today, very particularly in the West. The failure of the church to show to the world the unity that Christ has created is an act of deliberate disobedience. It is for the sake of his name that we should pray that Christians would be filled with a desire to worship together. In a large city it might be necessary to meet in a number of buildings, but all of those premises would be branches of the same Christian church, having the same name on the board outside: 'Church of Jesus Christ'. The style of worship might not be the same in each building, but our worship would still be an act of unity because each building would no longer be flying its own flag, but all would meet under the banner of Christ.

God blesses the parts of his church that are living in obedience to his prayer that they be one people. It has always been that way. The prophet Hosea could see it happening within the twin nations of Israel and Judah. The Lord explained this to Hosea: 'I will no longer show love to the house of Israel, that I should at all forgive them. Yet I will show love to the house of Judah; and I will save them' (Hosea 1:6–7). They were all God's people, in Israel and in Judah, but Israel dwindled to nothing while Judah prospered. It was a case of God distributing his blessing where the people were living in obedience to his word. Many parts of the continent of Africa are seeing revival while most towns in Britain and Ireland are seeing declining church attendance. Evangelism does not work unless there is unity. Billy Graham insists that all churches unite for his crusades, and so do many other less well-known evangelists. They know where the blessing lies.

The fact that God withdrew his blessing from Israel did not mean that all prayer stopped for that section of his people. Hosea kept on praying for the people of Israel. 'Return, O Israel, to the Lord your God…Say to him; "Forgive all our sins and receive us graciously"' (Hosea

14:1–2). The plight of the church in the West does not make us give up on prayer, but rather should make us more fervent in our intercession. The disobedient church is in need of prayer. A disobedient church is bad news. When it tries to preach the good news of the gospel the world pays no attention.

A former alcoholic once said to me: 'The most blessed place to be is rock bottom. When you have sunk so low that there are no lower depths to which you can sink, then you call to the Lord with the right intensity and out of a deep awareness of your need. That is the prayer that the Lord hears and answers.' Israel got to that state. It was like a hoard of locusts had descended on the land and eaten every green piece of vegetation until the land was stripped and there was nothing to eat. They had reached rock bottom. Then, 'when they had stripped the land clean, I cried out, "Sovereign Lord, forgive! How can Jacob survive? He is so small!"' (Amos 7:2). That was a heartfelt cry out of a state of desperate need. The Lord heard it and showed mercy and forgiveness.

It should be possible for the church to see its need and be aware of how desperate its situation is before it reaches rock bottom. The church in the West today needs to see its plight and to begin to pray for forgiveness. The tendency is to see the plight of the church but not to see any answer. The answer lies in repentance for the divisions and then pray earnestly for forgiveness and a willingness to unite.

Moving into the New Testament we find the Lord teaching his followers how to pray by giving them an outline prayer that has been repeated by Christian people all over the world ever since. It is almost a continuous prayer as you think of it ascending to the Father from someone's lips practically every moment of the day. 'Forgive us our debts, as we also have forgiven our debtors' (Matthew 6:12) becomes a prayer in the setting of the Lord's Prayer that needs to flow continuously from the hearts of us all. To receive and to give forgiveness has to be so prayed through that it eventually becomes a continuous experience in the life of every Christian. There must never be a moment when either unforgiveness or an unforgiven sin lies in our hearts, waiting for us to do something about it. The importance of continuously being in the spirit of true forgiveness is seen in the solemn words of Jesus that follow soon after the prayer: 'For if you forgive men when they sin against you, your heavenly Father will also forgive you. But if you do not forgive men their sins, your Father will not forgive your sins' (verses 14–15).

There is an authority that lies behind the act of forgiveness that we need to understand. To forgive is not a soft, sentimental act. It is an authoritative act and is spoken from strength and with conviction. When Jesus pronounced forgiveness to the paralysed man (Matthew 9:1–8) the crowd 'praised God, who had given such authority to men'. Jesus was saying that he had the authority to forgive sins and he spoke forgiveness out of that authority. But Jesus did not keep that authority to himself. He passed it on to his followers when he said: 'If you forgive anyone his sins, they are forgiven; if you do not forgive them, they are not forgiven' (John 20:23). Every Christian needs to enter into that God-given authority, to appropriate it, and to pronounce forgiveness from the heart.

The fact that forgiveness is a continuous process is also seen in the response to Peter's question: 'Lord, how many times shall I forgive my brother when he sins against me?' (Matthew 18:21). He tried answering his own question with a suggestion that there would come a time when forgiveness would stop, but in effect Jesus told him to stop counting. You do not count the number of sins committed against you; nor do you keep count of the number of times you have forgiven someone. Forgiveness is a continuous process. God is not keeping count of our wrongs or of how many times he has had to forgive us. Stop counting. Just let the forgiveness flow from you continuously.

There is a strong link between forgiveness and the Christian's prayer life. Whenever you sense that God is no longer answering your prayers, do a check-up to ensure that the process of continuous forgiveness has not dried up in your life. It was Jesus who forged the link between unanswered prayer and the failure to forgive. He said: 'When you stand praying, if you hold anything against anyone, forgive him, so that your Father in heaven may forgive you your sins' (Mark 11:25). Jesus is telling us that when we are praying and the continuous process of forgiveness has dried up in our hearts, we should stop praying. There is no point in continuing. God is not answering them. Even God has stopped forgiving that person because the process of forgiveness has to flow continuously from both the heart of the Christian and that of God at the same time. If one stops then both stop. Prayer becomes ineffective so it is better to stop praying and to get back into the flow of forgiveness, then praying may be resumed.

When the process of continuous forgiveness is flowing this does not mean that we are to condone the sin that is being forgiven. Jesus said: 'If your brother sins, rebuke him, and if he repents, forgive him. If he sins against you seven times in a day, and seven times comes back to you and says, "I repent," forgive him' (Luke 17:3–4). The sin has to be rebuked even as it is being forgiven. The sin is hated but the sinner is always loved. Keep that distinction clear between the sin and the sinner.

Peter takes us by surprise by using the word 'perhaps' in relation to God's forgiveness: 'Repent of this wickedness and pray to the Lord. Perhaps he will forgive you for having such a thought in your heart' (Acts 8:22). Peter was not presuming on God's forgiveness. When he was saying, 'Perhaps he will,' he was also saying, 'Perhaps he will not.' When is it necessary to use the word 'perhaps' in relation to God's forgiveness? The answer lies in what Peter saw in the heart of the man he was counselling: 'For I see that you are full of bitterness and captive to sin' (verse 23). Peter doubted if the man would repent of all the bitterness that was in his heart. The heart of the man created the 'perhaps' in Peter's vision of God's response.

A person who is held captive by sin does not feel the full weight of that sin until he begins to repent. None of us could stand the full weight of our sin, any more than Christ could bear the weight of our sin on the cross. It killed him. When repentance comes we begin to feel the weight of our sin, but because the repentance is followed by instant forgiveness from God, the weight is lifted. If we hesitate to forgive then we are leaving the person to feel the weight of their sin, and that may be more than they can bear.

Paul was aware of this danger when he wrote to the Christians at Corinth about one person who had sinned against the church but has since repented. He wrote: 'The punishment inflicted on him by the majority is sufficient for him. [They had put the man out of the church.] Now instead, you ought to forgive and comfort him, so that he will not be overwhelmed by excessive sorrow. I urge you, therefore, to reaffirm your love for him' (2 Corinthians 2:6–8). People can be overwhelmed by the act of repentance if it is not accompanied by immediate forgiveness from the Christians around them. God is faithful and never hesitates to forgive.

When Paul wrote: 'Forgive as the Lord forgave you' (Colossians 3:13) he said it all. God forgives perfectly. That is the ideal he sets before us. When it comes to forgiveness, do it Christ's way.

5

'Father, Forgive Them, for They Do Not Know What They Are Doing'

The Christian stands in awe of this cry from the lips of Jesus that comes ringing from the cross down through the ages. It is the most staggering act of forgiveness that the world has ever heard. It is a cry that deserves the fullest consideration. It needs to be understood in all its implications and in its most practical application to life today.

Although this is almost certainly the best known of the seven cries that came from the cross, it must be stated some have doubted whether Christ ever spoke the words. Students therefore have the right to challenge its authenticity and this is the first point to be dealt with in any serious consideration of the words.

Matthew, Mark and John make no reference to the cry when they record the events surrounding the crucifixion. There are a number of very early copies of Luke's gospel in existence, but these words of Jesus are not found in them all. The people who wrote out the copies of those manuscripts either deliberately omitted that statement or else they did not include it simply because it was not in the copy from which they were working. Against that, it must be said that some of the earliest manuscripts do contain this statement. That leaves it to the scholarship of the present-day translators of the Bible to decide whether the inclusion of this phrase is justified or not. Unanimously they have independently agreed that this cry from the cross is authentic and so it is included in all modern translations, though most editions publish a footnote to the effect that it is not found in all of the ancient manuscripts.

Once we are happy to go along with the view of the best scholarship of today and to accept these words of Jesus as authentic, then we can join the ranks of all the best Bible expositors and savour the richness and beauty of those words. The sermons they have inspired are without number and writers have let their pens run dry trying to show us how great is the heart of the One who could speak such overwhelming words from the depth of such terrible agony.

It is very unlikely that Luke was present at the cross to hear Jesus speak these words. He was a Gentile, not a Jew, and he wrote his account of the gospel for the benefit of fellow Gentiles. He engaged in years of research into the life of Jesus before putting pen to paper. He researched in Jerusalem, with James the Lord's brother, with Paul, in Capernaum, around Galilee. In fact everywhere he went he would have asked people if they had known Jesus and could tell him anything of the Teacher. He unearthed the most wonderful details about Jesus that the other gospel writers missed completely. How lovely that he found out about seven occasions when Jesus prayed that we would otherwise have known nothing about. His research certainly paid off when he discovered this saying of Jesus from the cross.

While everyone agrees that his plea for forgiveness was the first of the seven statements to come from the cross, it is a matter for conjecture as to when in that six-hour period the words were heard. Bishop J. C. Ryle and others have suggested that it would have been very early on, possibly as soon as the cross was raised and thrown into the hole prepared in the ground. It is possible that the words were spoken even as the nails were being driven into his hands or feet, that they came forth from that moment of intense agony. It is even possible that Christ prayed the prayer more than once over those six hours. The prayer for forgiveness flows continuously from the heart of Jesus. The Father must be hearing it as a constant plea right through our lifetime for 'Christ Jesus, who died—more than that, who was raised to life—is at the right hand of God and is also interceding for us' (Romans 8:34).

Our lives are to echo that prayer continuously. It is to be our constant theme as we see people inflict dreadful suffering on each other. It should flow from our hearts as clearly as it did from the heart of Stephen as the stones crashed off his body in death-dealing blows—'Then he fell on his knees and cried out, "Lord, do not hold this sin against them"' (Acts 7:60).

We must be careful not to narrow Christ's prayer down so as to refer only to a small group of people. It was not just the Roman soldiers for whom he prayed as they drove in the nails. The compassion of Christ was far greater than that. He was concerned for the whole Jewish nation; for all the Jews who had cried out that morning, 'Crucify him.' This can be seen in the way he phrased the prayer: 'They do not know what they are doing.' This is a phrase that needs to be carefully interpreted. It is a plea based on the ignorance of the people. In secular law the plea of ignorance bears no weight. If I am travelling at 60 mph in a 40 mph speed limit area, it is no use for me to plead ignorance—'I did not know it was a speed limit area.' It was my business to know, to observe the warning sign posts. The highway code and every other law is there to be learned and observed. Ignorance is no plea.

In the law of Christ's kingdom, when praying for the people who had sent him to the cross, Jesus felt it right to use the plea of ignorance. The people did not know he was the Messiah. Perhaps they should have known. The signs were there for them to read in the miracles he performed and the teaching he gave. Certainly the high priest, Caiaphas, had no excuse. He could not plead ignorance. He had asked the direct question: 'Tell us if you are the Christ, the Son of God,' and Jesus gave a direct answer: 'Yes, it is as you say' (Matthew 26:63–64).

But there was ignorance among both Roman soldiers and the Jewish crowd. The whole concept of Jesus as Messiah was beyond the ability of their finite minds to accept. He did not fit in to their preconceived ideas at all. A rejected Messiah was out of the question. Christ recognized this dilemma and made a plea for their ignorance to be taken into consideration.

The plea of ignorance does not mean that the act committed is no longer a sin. It means that there is an added reason to go with grace and mercy why pardon might be granted. It is a plea for forgiveness for the sin committed, never a plea of innocence.

Paul could see this as he thought of the people responsible for the sin of sending Christ to the cross. He wrote: 'None of the rulers of this age understood it, for if they had, they would not have crucified the Lord of glory' (1 Corinthians 2:8). Paul then took that truth and applied it to his own life and situation—'Even though I was once a blasphemer and a persecutor and a violent man, I was shown mercy because I acted in ignorance and unbelief' (1 Timothy 1:13).

Then Paul goes on to state the grounds on which he was forgiven, and ignorance was not listed in that case. Ignorance could be used as a basis on which to ask for pardon, but he knew that the forgiveness he received was based on much greater qualities—'The grace of our Lord was poured out on me abundantly, along with the faith and love that are in Christ Jesus' (verse 14). Grace, faith and love are the qualities from where forgiveness comes. The grace of God is sufficient for every occasion. There is no area where a sin could be committed that is beyond the grace of God. Christ knew that and he had the faith to believe it. He could ask a father to forgive the people who were killing that father's only son. He could do that because the father was his Father, and Jesus knew the grace of his Father. The third quality of love is of equal significance to those of grace and faith. It was the love of the Father that caused him to give his only Son to the cross (John 3:16). It was the love of the Son that made him willing to go to the cross. Those three qualities are supreme. There is none greater. They flow from the cross in continuous forgiveness.

It is no wonder that Bible expositors have waxed so eloquent on these twelve words from the cross. W. Phillip Keller who has written so graphically of the 23rd Psalm and other passages of the Scriptures in *Rabboni* (Fleming M. Revell 1977), has commented on this cry of Jesus:

> A more incredible cry has never come from any lips. Instead of vituperation or vehemence, here was God revealed. Here was the character of Christ in colours so vivid no man could ever mistake them. Such forgiveness!

You can almost see the Father hurrying to answer that prayer. It echoes his own heart so perfectly. There is no request he is more willing to grant than the desire for forgiveness. Look at the thief on the cross turning to Christ in his physical agony and crying for mercy. See the look in those dying eyes as he hears the gentle answer of promise coming from the parched and bleeding lips of Jesus. There in that moment Jesus and the thief both received the answer to Christ's prayer.

Look down at the foot of the cross and see a Roman centurion watch the last dying breath escape from the lips of Jesus. See the Father touch his heart and change his whole attitude to the One he had just executed. Listen as he speaks with a sincerity he never knew he possessed, and say it loud enough for someone to hear, someone who would later repeat the sentence to Luke: 'Surely this was a righteous man.' Did the spirit of Jesus hear those words, that answer to his prayer, as it slipped away from his body to await the resurrected body?

Stand in the streets of Jerusalem at Pentecost and hear the good news of the kingdom being proclaimed in the full power of the newly-received Holy Spirit by Peter, and watch as some 3,000 people respond with a full acceptance of all the forgiveness that the kingdom provides. The Father at that moment was answering the prayer of his Son.

Watch the continued spread of the gospel in Jerusalem during the following months, see priests whose whole adult lives had been devoted to the shedding of the blood of innocent lambs in order to dispense forgiveness to the people, suddenly recognize the Lamb of God on the cross and receive a cleansing and forgiveness they had never dreamed possible: 'A large number of priests became obedient to the faith' (Acts 6:7). Thank you, Father, for answering the prayer of Jesus.

Every Christian man, woman and child who today is receiving and dispensing forgiveness is a living witness to the Father's answer to the prayer from the cross. A prayer of that magnitude demands an answer that is continuous, that never ceases to flow and to be received. To reject the forgiveness of God, to refuse to forgive someone who has wronged us, is to deny the cry from the cross, to spurn the plea of Jesus.

Herbert Lockyer traced the events of Easter in a slim but a vividly-written volume called *The Week that Changed the World* (Pickering & Inglis). When he came to the cross he wrote:

> There has never been a preacher like the dying Christ, no pulpit like the cross, no congregation like the one present at Calvary, no sermon like the seven sayings of Jesus in the hours of his anguish.

King David, in the throes of composition as he strummed the strings of his harp, received a revelation from the Father that was beyond his comprehension. It spoke of Calvary, the Son and the cross. All he could do was write them down with a tremulous hand and softly sing them with trembling lips: 'I can count all my bones; people stare and gloat over me. They divide my garments among them and cast lots for my clothing' (Psalm 22:17–18). If those words were fulfilled in their entirety it is inconceivable that the words Jesus prayed from the cross would not also be fulfilled. You can see the fulfilment in people's lives all over the world, even though sometimes there is also rejection.

Charles H. Spurgeon kept notes of the sermons he preached at the Tabernacle in London that later came to bear his name. He must have waxed eloquent when he preached on this text. His notes simply state: 'Forgiveness is the first, chief and basic blessing. Forgiveness from the Father can even go so far as to pardon the murder of His Son' *My Sermon Notes* (Passmore and Alabaster 1896). With that slip of paper in front of him Spurgeon had no problem in filling sixty minutes of exhortation for people to respond to the forgiveness of God.

Matthew, Mark and John could afford to omit this cry from the cross when writing their accounts of the gospel, but it was different for Luke. He was writing to the governor of a Roman province, a pagan unbeliever called Theophilus. Would that cry from the cross reach the heart of a Roman governor the way it had to the soul of a Roman centurion?

Luke addressed his pagan friend with the respect due to a man of his standing in the empire: 'Most excellent Theophilus' (Luke 1:3). When Luke came to write his second great report, the Acts of the Apostles, he was sending it to the same man but it would seem that his friend had lost his place of power. He no longer had a title. He was simply 'Theophilus' (Acts 1:1). Had the reading of Luke's gospel resulted in him becoming a believer, receiving the forgiveness that flowed from the cross, so that he was no longer considered a fit person to rule in a pagan empire? Had the prayer of Jesus been answered in his life also?

The name Theophilus means 'Lover of God'. What a glorious name for a man who once tried to love gods of stone but who later came to love the God who loved him enough to forgive him of all his sins. Everyone who lives in an unbelieving world needs to be armed with this cry from the cross, this message of forgiveness. It can melt the hearts of all who hear it.

6

The Woman Caught in Adultery

The early morning encounter in the temple between Jesus and the woman caught in the act of adultery (John 8:1–11) provides a glorious insight into the character of Jesus and into the role of the forgiver when faced with the religious laws of the day. Before we even consider the incident, however, we must be clear that this is an historical event and not the figment of someone's vivid imagination. The doubts surrounding this incident are far stronger than those surrounding Christ's first cry from the cross.

It needs no great feat of scholarship to discover that the story of the encounter with the adulteress is not to be found in any of the oldest copies of John's gospel. All of the modern translators are agreed on this. They have chosen various methods to indicate to the reader that there is a doubt whether this incident really took place. Some have printed the passage in brackets. Others have lifted it out of the gospel and printed it at the end with a note of explanation. At the very least each modern translator would print a footnote stating that the incident is not to be found in the earliest manuscripts.

If such an incident did take place, Matthew, Mark and Luke make no reference to it. If this great act of forgiveness on the part of Jesus is to be any help to us we need to free ourselves first of any doubts as to its authenticity. For years scholars have minutely studied this problem and they are to be commended for their exhaustive research. Let us simply gather up the cream of their findings and benefit from it, thankful that such great minds have done all the hard work for us.

There is a general agreement that John did not record this incident in his account of the ministry of Jesus—but that in no way indicates that it never happened. John continually had to make a selection of what to record and what to omit. The three years of public ministry in which Christ engaged were so packed with teaching and miracles that John had to admit: 'Jesus did many other things as well. If every one of them were written down, I suppose that even the whole world would not have room for the books that would be written' (John 21:25). Let us start by accepting that the meeting with the adulteress was one of the 'other things' that happened but which John chose to leave out.

Next let us accept that what Jesus is reported to have said and done in this incident is completely true to his character. In fact we might well say that no one but Jesus would ever have behaved in this way under such circumstances. So we are saying with the scholars that this incident would be completely true to character and we could well believe that it did take place. In fact it is easier to believe that than to think it was the figment of someone's imagination.

For years after the ascension of Jesus people would be passing on by word of mouth things they had heard Jesus say and do. A man called Papias, a disciple of John who rose to a leadership position in the church in the first half of the second century, started writing down these oral traditions so as to keep a record of them. This was a very valuable work that he undertook. As a disciple of John he would naturally take a particular interest in reading his master's account of the life of Jesus. He would be aware of the wealth of material that John had to omit and he might well do what many a disciple did—reading a passage like

John 8:15, 'You judge by human standards; I pass judgement on no-one,' he would recall the story he heard and wrote down of Jesus meeting the adulteress and would see how wonderfully it illustrated this saying of Jesus about passing judgement. It would be natural for a disciple under such circumstances to write the incident in the margin of the manuscript. It would need only one scribe after that, when copying the manuscript, to move the incident out of the margin and place it in the text, for it to become part of John's gospel.

This theory by the scholars is one that appeals to me. I can picture it happening without any difficulty and I know that similar insertions have occurred many times in the world of early literature. The scholars are therefore saying that John may not have recorded this incident. It is very likely that the meeting took place exactly as recorded. Someone else, thinking it was too good to omit, wrote it in. Papias would be the most likely known person to have done this. Let us therefore accept the ruling of the best in scholarship and agree that the incident is authentic.

Now let us learn about forgiveness in this meeting between Jesus and this 'prodigal daughter'. Her name is not given so her identity is not important. This could be anyone caught in the act of sinning. It was early morning, the dawn was just breaking. Jesus had spent the night in the Mount of Olives, as he often did when in the vicinity of Jerusalem. So often Jesus had nowhere to lay his head. As soon as he appeared in the temple a crown gathered round him. He sat down and started to teach them. In the East a teacher would always take a sitting position. When Jesus had a proclamation to make, like a herald, he stood up (John 7:37), but when he was teaching he sat down.

A teacher does not like to be interrupted in the middle of his discourse, but the Pharisees and lawyers had no hesitation in breaking up this lesson. They pushed through the crowd and threw a woman into the middle of the assembly.

I wonder, had they been on their way to the Sanhedrin

that met in a nearby section of the temple? There they could officially bring their charge against the woman. When they saw Jesus in session they seized the opportunity to challenge him with a trick question. According to the law of Moses anyone caught committing adultery was to be stoned to death, and that applied to both the man and the woman in the case. When the Roman Empire took over Israel they forbade the Jews to sentence anyone to death or to execute anyone. That was why only the Romans could sentence Jesus and crucify him.

The test for Jesus in the case of this woman was that if he said: 'Let her go free,' he would be speaking against the law of Moses. If he said: 'Stone her to death,' he would be disobeying the law of Rome. In either case the lawyers could bring a charge against him. It seemed a golden opportunity with a crowd of people to witness Jesus falling into a trap.

Jesus was also well up in his knowledge of the law. There were no courts of law in those days. Anyone seeing a person committing an offence could take the offender to the city gate and there the appropriate sentence for the offence could be carried out. The only question to be decided was the reliability of the witnesses, and who dare question the reliability of Pharisees and lawyers?

Jesus knew that the law stipulated that if the fitting punishment was for the offender to be stoned to death then the witnesses must always throw the first stones (Deuteronomy 17:7). He also knew that if true justice was to be done then the man should have been brought there as well as the woman.

Jesus was also very aware that in the hearts of these accusers was the desire to see him stoned to death. They were much more interested in the execution of Jesus than they were in the death of the unfortunate woman.

Jesus showed his complete disdain of the whole proceedings, his desire to continue teaching the people and his refusal to become involved in such distasteful trickery as this, by refusing to answer the question. He did not even look at the accusers. He doodled in the dust with a stick as though he had not heard their question.

Commentators have had great fun making guesses at what Jesus was doing with the stick, or with his finger, in the dust. I would suggest that if the writing on the ground had any significance at all we would have been told what was written. The Holy Spirit, who inspired all Scripture, would have brought it to the mind of the recorder to report what Jesus wrote. The Holy Spirit does not leave it to our guesswork to find out the truth. Rather, we should see the bowed head of Jesus, the scribbling on the ground, as a mark of his stated indifference to the whole proceedings. He could see through it like looking through a window, and he wanted no part in it.

The silence of those moments must have infuriated the Pharisees. They were not used to being ignored. The crowd was spellbound, watching his every move. It was getting embarrassing for the Pharisees. The woman must have been holding her breath.

The feast of tabernacles had just ended the previous day. The city streets were crowded with people. Immorality was a common scene everywhere. Jesus was living in 'a wicked and adulterous generation' (Matthew 12:39). His plan was to bring salvation to sinners, not to sentence them to death.

The Pharisees tried desperately to stop the situation from slipping out of their control. They kept questioning Jesus, demanding an answer, hanging on like terriers. I wonder how long Jesus ignored them. Eventually he took up the challenge, surely for the benefit of the woman as much as for any other reason, straightened up and made that profound statement to the accusers: 'If any one of you is without sin, let him be the first to throw a stone at her' (verse 7). Jesus never suggested that the woman was innocent. He raised the question as to who, among everyone present, was fit to be her judge and executioner. The only possible answer was: 'Jesus.' He was the only person present who was without sin. This is the only place in the New Testament where this phrase 'without sin' is used. It means 'sinless'. It means Jesus.

Having delivered that bulls-eye shot, Jesus resumed his annoying stance of having nothing to do with this sordid business—he stooped down and began doodling on the ground again.

The scene changed. The Pharisees were no longer asking their questions. They were silenced. Jesus waited and waited. Then he looked up. The crowd, his listening audience, was sitting in stunned silence. One by one, the Pharisees and lawyers had slipped away. The woman was still standing in the middle of the crowd, waiting for someone to become her judge.

For the second time Jesus straightened up. This time his eyes were looking at the woman. He called to her: 'Woman.' That is how Jesus called to his mother when he looked at her from the cross. That is how he spoke to the other Mary on the morning of his resurrection. It must have sounded so full of compassion.

He asked her two questions: 'Where are they? Has no-one condemned you?' She then spoke for the first and only time: 'No-one, sir.'

Then came the judgement from the sinless judge: 'Then neither do I condemn you. Go now and leave your life of sin.'

Let us quickly answer any mind that is querying how Jesus could forgive sin when he had not yet died on the cross for the sin of the world. Let it never be forgotten that John refers to Jesus as 'the Lamb that was slain from the creation of the world' (Revelation 13:8). The reality of the atonement is an ever-present truth in the heart of God.

When Jesus said: 'Leave your life of sin,' he was expressing the power that lies behind the act of forgiveness. Forgiveness releases people from the power of sin. If that woman had never been able to resist the sin of adultery before, she was certainly able to do so after she experienced the forgiveness of Jesus. From that moment on the sin would appear so distasteful, so horrible, to her that it would be no trouble to resist it.

Take this precious incident from the life of Jesus and let it reveal to you that sinners, even saved sinners, are never to be judges who condemn other sinners. Only the sinless One may pronounce condemnation. None other may. Our hearts must reflect the heart of Jesus in all things. We must forgive as he forgives, and in forgiving release the person we forgive from the power of the sin that has crippled them. Only true genuine forgiveness carries this power within it. What is genuine forgiveness? It is the forgiveness that carries not a trace of condemnation. 'Neither do I condemn you,' says the sinless One.

7

A Christian Ulsterman

Anyone born outside Northern Ireland may find it hard to understand the extent to which the place of birth shapes the mentality and attitudes of the average Ulsterman. You inevitably become what you are born into. These next two chapters will show the extent to which this is true from Protestant and Catholic points of view, and how someone can emerge out of that narrowing mould while remaining rooted in the life of the community and the church. The two men concerned in these chapters would once have sat in judgement on each other. The woman in the last chapter showed us that none of us is in a position to condemn another person. We will now see how these two men have escaped from the attitude of condemnation.

Take the case of a Presbyterian minister born in Belfast. Protestantism and Presbyterianism are closely associated in people's minds in Northern Ireland. Although Presbyterianism expresses itself in five separate denominations in Northern Ireland, in the eyes of a Catholic they each portray Protestantism at its staunchest. The Church of Ireland (part of the Anglican Communion) is not seen as being quite so militant in its Protestant stand as is Presbyterianism.

The Rev Ken Newell, minister of Fitzroy Presbyterian

Church in University Street, Belfast, since 1976, can see how clearly his life was shaped for him in his early days. He would probably have continued uncritically within that mould had it not been for several years of missionary service in Indonesia under the Overseas Board of the Presbyterian Church in Ireland. Going abroad has the effect of helping the Ulsterman emerge from the restricting influences of his background. But even that experience overseas can be of no avail if the person's mind is not open to learn from other people with other points of view.

Ken Newell was born on the Shore Road, Belfast in May, 1943. That means he was born in a strongly loyalist area where growing up without meaningful relationships with Roman Catholics would be considered normal. Opportunities to play with Catholic children were rare because very few Catholics were living in his area, and none to his knowledge attended Seaview Primary School where he was a pupil. This situation of unconscious social apartheid was often carried into the schools, since loyalists attended State schools which were predominantly Protestant, while Catholics attended schools of their own denomination. For children of different traditions to grow up apart from each other was natural.

Ken's first meaningful relationship with a Catholic happened as a result of his fervent teenage support of Crusaders football club. He had a trial match with the youth team and every Saturday without fail he would attend matches both at home and away. One Saturday afternoon, on the terraces at Seaview, where Crusaders played, one of the supporters of the club was pointed out to Ken as being a Catholic, as though that made him different. However, the fact that he wore a black and red scarf ensured that his football allegiance overcame even religious prejudice, and later Ken and Jim, as he was called, became good friends and visited each other's homes.

The most important community ritual to which young children are introduced is the collection of wood for the bonfire on the eleventh night of July each year. Everyone would be involved, but young people have a special part to play. This annual celebration recalls the Battle of the Boyne in 1690 which is interpreted in the popular mind as the Protestants under King William of Orange defeating the Catholics under King James near Drogheda. On top of the bonfire the young people would place an effigy of the Pope and watch it being consumed by the raging flames. It is a common practice among the Protestant community, when feelings are running high, to set on fire any hate-symbols. German youth had anti-Semitism fed into their minds during the rise of Nazism when similar bonfires burned the hate-symbol of a Jew. Young people unconsciously accept such customs and in so doing have their minds shaped as they collect the wood, stuff an effigy and set fire to it. In the middle of the fun, feasting and celebrations of the evening their minds are being nurtured in suspicion, dislike and then even hatred of the very symbols that Roman Catholics respect and revere. Religious bigotry is often minted at the fires on the eleventh night.

Part of the festivities would include the singing of anti-Catholic songs. The younger children would learn these by heart as they listened to them being sung by older teenagers with pride and much feeling in their voices. These songs would reinforce the attitudes already being created by the bonfires, and frequently expressed scathing references to the Pope, the Virgin Mary and the Catholic community. They expressed a religious and political contempt for the 'other side' and at the same time revealed a racial pride and sense of superiority on the part of those who sang them. Similar songs and community rituals exist on the Catholic nationalist side and they have the same effect.

Catholics in Northern Ireland are often referred to as Fenians. It is a name steeped in history, just like the Battle of the Boyne. Although an Irish-American society took the name Fenian for themselves between 1863 and 1870, it really goes back to Finn MacCumhaill, leader of a legendary band of Irish robbers. To call a Catholic a Fenian meant you were calling him an enemy, someone out to get rid of British rule in Ireland.

Because of the strength of family life in Ulster many children pick up biased attitudes from simply talking with their parents at meal times. Parents will recall vivid memories from the past in which Catholics were involved, and the natural conclusion for a young mind to draw from such stories is: 'You can never trust a Catholic. He may smile at you to your face, but in a crisis he will stab you in the back.' This is what comes of living in a country where conflict has been a part of life for centuries. The Ulsterman has a strong 'enemy consciousness' from early in life. The supreme value is to be loyal to your tribe and your fore-fathers, whatever side they may have been on.

Ken was baptized and brought up within a local Presbyterian church where Sunday School work was very strong, Boys' Brigade and Girls' Brigade flourished and where the Bible was taught on Sundays within a warmly evangelical atmosphere. It seemed natural in such an environment to move towards faith in Jesus Christ and a love for the Scriptures. At seventeen Ken became a communicant in the church by profession of faith. Looking back on this upbringing he can now see some of the weaknesses that emerged. All references to the Roman Catholic church and community tended to be highly selective and negative, pinpointing the faults in the system while ignoring the obvious strengths that it contains and its outstanding Christian personalities. The doctrines that were considered in error were highlighted, and no recognition was given to such fundamental Christian doctrines as the virgin birth, the sinless life of Christ, the atoning death, the resurrection and the second coming. There was an uncritical acceptance of loyalist attitudes so that the gospel would rarely be allowed to touch on the prejudices that were expressed in their community rituals. It was a sin to smoke, but not to burn the symbol of another man's faith. It was a sin to have a drink, but not to be completely one-sided in political loyalties.

Seventeen was also the age at which Ken joined his local branch of the Orange Order. His sponsors for membership were some pleasant loyalist neighbours who, though they did not attend church, thought it was good for young people to join an Order that would defend Protestantism and the union with Britain. It was also the time when Ken left Belfast High School and went to study classics at Queen's University, Belfast. During those university years he felt that God was calling him towards the ministry of the Presbyterian church in Ireland. This became known within the Lodge, and as a result he was promoted to the position of chaplain there, opening the meetings with prayer and a reading from Scripture. The members also asked him to undertake a study of the origins and basis of the Orange Order and at each meeting to instruct them in the principles of Orangeism.

Most members of the Lodge were decent, hardworking men who had friendships with Catholics mainly through their work, but some were decidedly sectarian and viewed the Catholic community as a threat, the Catholic Church as the whore of Babylon and the Pope as the anti-Christ.

In October 1964 Ken went into the Presbyterian college at Botanic Avenue to study theology and to prepare for the ministry. At that time he was opposed to the ecumenical movement because he saw it as a threat to Protestantism with its open attitude to the Roman Catholic Church. He was opposed to the World Council of Churches because it was the voice of the ecumenical movement. In his last year at college he decided to make a personal in-depth study of this 'enemy' from the inside, so he applied to the WCC for a scholarship. In 1967 he was offered a scholarship to continue his New Testament studies at Ridley Hall, Cambridge and so came to live within an Anglican evangelical community and to study under Professor C. F. D. Moule at the Divinity School. This also gave him the opportunity to meet theological lecturers from different parts of the world and from traditions that ranged from Baptist to Greek Orthodox. It was there also that he met Anglicans who were both evangelical and ecumenical as well as some, like the Rev Michael Harper, who had come into the experience of spiritual renewal.

Part of the scholarship included a study of the Dutch Catholic Church which in the 1960s was considered very progressive. At Easter 1968, with a team of theological students from all over the United Kingdom, he went to Amsterdam and stayed in a Catholic hostel near a large Roman Catholic university. During that time he also attended the Dutch Reform college at Driebergen where Catholic and Reformed theologians presented papers on how the church should relate to the community and share the good news of Christ. This was the first time that Ken had sat under the teaching of Catholic theologians. He was astonished to discover that the Catholic lecturers were reasoning from Scripture with more conviction than their Dutch Reformed counterparts who were more liberal.

Another experience was to attend a Catholic folk Mass in Amsterdam. Students were free to decide whether to attend or not. Having imbibed from his own background that the Mass was a blasphemy against the Person of Christ because it tried to sacrifice him afresh at each celebration, Ken was hesitant about attending. He decided to go as a detached and critical observer and sat at the back of the large university church to watch what was happening. This was something he would never have dared to do in Belfast in case anyone saw him going in or out of the church. To his surprise he was impressed by the beauty, dignity, reverence and Christ-centred joy of the service. There was an orchestra to lead the fervent praise and the congregational participation was enthusiastic and worshipful. The officiating priest wore an ordinary shirt and tie. Both bread and wine were offered to the people and approximately 1,000 participated.

After the celebration he sat in a local restaurant with a group of students and probed them about what had been happening in the Mass. Many of them confessed that they had gone to meet with the once crucified but now risen Christ who was spiritually present but not physically present in the elements. Ken was coming to realize that their view of the Eucharist was not too far distant from his view of what happened at Communion within the average Presbyterian church. The joy of the celebration contrasted with the frequently heavy sombreness of the Lord's Supper within his own tradition.

Ken had not participated in the Eucharist but his outlook on the Catholic Church was changing. What he was seeing did not match with what he had heard about the Catholic Mass at home.

On his return to Ireland in July 1968 Ken took up his role as Assistant Minister at Hamilton Road Presbyterian Church in the seaside resort of Bangor. It was at the Christmas of that year that he was married in St John's Presbyterian Church, Newtownbreda, Belfast. During his last months in Cambridge, aware that ordination was not very far away, Ken felt the need to be completely and exclusively dedicated to Christ and to his church and to have no direct semi-political allegiance to another cause. He did not want to be wearing an Orange vest under his clerical shirt but rather to be free to serve Christ and the whole community in Northern Ireland. He sent off his resignation to the local Lodge and left the Orange Order. He was unhappy about membership of the Order because he could see the danger of it narrowing down political loyalties to sectarianism and limiting the biblical view of the church to denominationalism.

Most leaders in the Orange Order would be mystified by Ken's decision and would not understand it. It is the outsider looking on who can often see most clearly how the Orange Order, like Freemasonry, can often become first priority in a man's life unconsciously relegating loyalty to Jesus Christ, his teaching and his church to second place.

Ken wanted to move freely in every section of the Northern Ireland community as a servant of Christ offering friendship without any fences.

Everyone ordained into the Presbyterian church in Ireland is obliged to sign the Westminster Confession of Faith as a standard subordinate to the supreme authority of Scripture. The Confession includes the following statement: 'The Pope of Rome is that anti-Christ, that man of sin, and son of perdition that exalteth himself in the Church against Christ, and all that is called God' (Chapter 25 section six). The Confession defines Reformed theology over against the teaching of the Roman Catholic Church and is helpful in pinpointing areas of religious controversy. However, Ken could see that in identifying the Pope as the anti-Christ it goes beyond Scripture, as its weak reference to biblical texts at that point clearly showed.

Professor Charles Hodge of Princeton Theological Seminary, probably the greatest Reformed theologian of the last century, was also conscious that the Confession overstated its case at points. In July, 1867 he wrote an article in the Princeton Review entitled, 'What is meant by adopting the Westminster Confession?' Early in the article he writes:

> There are many propositions contained in the Westminster Confession which do not belong to the integrity of the Reformed system. A man may be a true Calvinist and not believe that the Pope is the anti-Christ predicted by St Paul.

Professor Hodge's position on the Confession of Faith is that which has characterized historical Presbyterianism, namely that each phrase and word of the Confession was never meant to be binding on those who signed it. Rather it is the pattern of Reformed theology underlying the Confession to which ministers pledge their support in their ordination vows. From Ken's point of view he saw that these words relating to the Pope were biblically unjustified, spiritually unbalanced and morally unfair.

As Ken entered the 1970s he was still emerging from Ulster fundamentalism and sectarianism. Violence was erupting all over Ulster at that time. He was preparing to find a congregation of his own in which he could express his loyalty to Christ and continue his involvement in the life of the Presbyterian church. He had completed his Master of Theology degree at Queens when an invitation came from the Overseas Board of the Presbyterian church to consider teaching New Testament Theology at the Theological Academy of the Christian Evangelical church in Timor, Indonesia. This was to be the experience that would melt away the last remaining vestiges of prejudice and bring him into a much wider vision of the church, the Holy Spirit and the need for world evangelization.

From 1965 Indonesia had experienced a great out-pouring of the Holy Spirit in the area to which he was called and it in fact became known as the 'Timor Revival'. During this time the church at Timor was growing at the rate of 22,000 members a year. Ken had read about revivals in the past, but now he was to be present at the tail end of a very significant one. In a revival the church experiences a kind of spiritual resurrection that enables the life and power of Christ to be expressed to the people. It was in this setting that Ken began to see what a deeper obedience to Christ might mean for him.

In preparation for this missionary work in Indonesia the Overseas Board sent him and his family in 1971 to study all that is Indonesian at the Dutch Reformed Missionary College near Leiden. In studying the culture of Indonesia, and the ways in which people are moulded by their communities, Ken began to rethink how the culture of Ulster also moulds the attitudes of its people. He began to see that the purpose of the gospel is to transform culture, eroding what is arrogant and biased and filling the positive aspects with the love of Christ. At this point Ken would quote 1 Peter 1:18–19, 'It was not with perishable things such as silver or gold that you were *redeemed from the empty way of life handed down to you from your forefathers*, but with the precious blood of Christ' (italics his).

In July 1972 the Newells left Ireland for Indonesia, visiting on the way other Presbyterian missionaries working in Beirut and Bombay. Everywhere he went he was meeting local Christian leaders and overseas missionaries of all traditions whose view of the church was wider and richer than his own, and whose congregations were growing through evangelism and positive social concern. He saw ecumenical convictions flowing out of hearts that were joyfully and truly evangelical. This combination was new to him and largely unknown in Northern Ireland where the church is polarized as well as sheltered from the major currents of world Christianity. The Indonesian Christians clearly believed that the unity of the church is at the heart of the gospel.

In September 1972 Ken was appointed to the position of lecturer in New Testament studies in the Theological Academy at Kupang. On the staff were four Indonesian lecturers and a Dutch Reformed Old Testament lecturer. The church in Timor enjoyed ecumenical relationships with the Presbyterian and Methodist Churches in Australia, the Lutheran church in Germany, the Dutch Reformed Church and the Presbyterian Church in Ireland. At the college about 100 students were preparing for the ministry, of whom about one-fifth were women.

The Theological Academy was just ten miles outside Kupang, the capital city of Timor, and down into the city came Roman Catholic priests seeking a rest from the primitive interior of the island. Many of the priests were Irish, working with the Society of the Divine Word, and when they head that an Irish missionary had arrived they began dropping into the Newell's home to welcome them and have a chat. One priest in particular became a very close friend to Ken and was a regular visitor at their home. He was Fr Noel Carroll from Dundalk in Ireland, whose parish in Timor was in one of the remotest and deprived parts of the island. His dedication to the people and the way in which he shared in their poverty and suffering led Ken to see him as a male counterpart to Mother Theresa of Calcutta. Many evenings at the Newell's home were devoted to discussions on the theological differences between Protestantism and Catholicism, as well as the increasing number of areas in which a common faith was emerging. Slowly out of this heart-to-heart friendship Ken began to see that Christ was as much present in Noel's life and as much Noel's Lord and Saviour as he was his. Slowly the conclusion formed in his mind that the two of them were not strangers but fellow citizens of God's kingdom.

During the time at Timor there were serious flooding and several epidemics of cholera throughout the island. Ken was impressed to see nuns, priests, ministers and evangelists all caring for each other's communities without any reservations, ministering to each other materially and spiritually as though they were all part of the one flock. How different, Ken reflected, from the situation in Northern Ireland, where priests and ministers can live close by each other and yet rarely cross each other's doorsteps. It was easy for him to see which situation was the closest to the teaching of Jesus.

Ken was seeing what Irish people as a whole so desperately need to realize, that anyone who truly owns Jesus Christ as Lord is a brother or sister in Christ, even though there may be important doctrinal differences between them. He is still aware of the differences that exist between the two traditions, but he also sees that what they have in common in Christ is sufficient to make them all part of God's one family. Once that is realized it becomes possible to talk about the differences in a spirit of love and to learn from each other.

Shortly before taking his furlough in June 1975 a letter was received by the Principal of the Theological Academy at Kupang from the Catholic Theological college on the neighbouring island of Flores which trained priests for work throughout south-east Asia. The Catholic college requested that one of the Reformed lecturers should be released to take part in the training of those future priests. They were asking for a lecturer in the New Testament, so Ken was appointed to teach for a month in the Catholic college. He began preparing material on Paul's letter to the Galatians with its strong teaching on justification by grace through faith. The Theological Academy asked that the Catholic college should in return provide someone to lecture on philosophy, this being an important part of the curriculum for traditional Catholic training for the ministry. Once again Ken was comparing the freedom within the evangelical Third World churches to be open in the realm of theological training and the hesitancy to be similarly involved at home in Ireland. He could not help feeling that such openness was closer to the spirit of Christ than the cold theological suspicions generated over centuries in Ireland. There were 150 Catholic priests at the seminary to which he was invited, but in fact the approach of his furlough prevented him from going and a Dutch Reformed colleague took his place.

When the time came for him to go home on furlough in June 1975 he was a different person from the time he had left Ireland. He realized that many of the students he had been teaching would never have got to the college to be trained as ministers or evangelists if they had not received scholarships from the Indonesian Council of Churches via the World Council of Churches. Ken was now no longer an anti-Catholic Ulsterman. He could see how impoverished such attitudes could be. He was becoming more strongly evangelical in his theological convictions and also more ecumenical in his appreciation of the worldwide nature of Christ's church. This had all happened through living with the church overseas. It reminded him of what a former professor of the Presbyterian college in Belfast used to say to the students: 'When you go overseas you always come back home to the house next door.'

During the furlough in Belfast from July to Christmas 1975 their plans to return to Indonesia for another term of service were dashed when unforeseen medical problems turned them in a new direction. Missionary work overseas was now out of the question and Ken began thinking of how to serve Christ within his own country. So it was that in January 1976 he became the minister of Fitzroy Presbyterian Church in Belfast, near to Queen's University where he had studied. The church had welcomed members from two other Presbyterian churches that had closed down, Donegall Pass and Crescent, raising the number of families to about 600. The Botanic area served by the church was slowly changing. It had always been a mixed population of Catholics and Protestants and the relationships had been relatively good. Now the older Protestant families were dying off and younger Catholic families were moving in from areas of Belfast that had bad housing or had experienced conflict. Fitzroy had a reputation for being a warmhearted evangelical congregation. For 100 years it had been served by four distinguished ministries.

Shortly after Ken took over at Fitzroy the Peace Movement broke out in Belfast. He and a considerable number of elders and members became involved, attending the large public rallies and more local activities. As a result of local initiatives between four different churches in the area (Presbyterian, Church of Ireland, Congregational and Roman Catholic) a Christmas carol service was held in the open air in December 1977. It had to be held outside because both Catholic and Protestant churches were sensitive about inviting each other into their buildings. Torrential rain fell throughout the Sunday afternoon service, but it did not dampen the joy and love that was felt by the hundred people who met for the first service of its kind in the Botanic area.

During this time Ken formed a close friendship with the Roman Catholic priest for the Botanic area, Fr Denis

Newberry. They met quite often to discuss their ministries, to plan joint ventures, visit each other's churches and just be good friends. They would often be seen walking round the area together and their obvious friendship in Christ broadcast a message far clearer than any spoken word could have done. The carol service continued for several years with up to 400 people coming together. At one of those services held in Fitzroy Church, with the place crammed full of people from both sides of the community, Ken felt so much joy at the sight that he wept silent tears of thanksgiving. He had never witnessed anything like this before.

Working for reconciliation in Belfast can be a daunting task, with many disappointments, considerable resistance and opposition as well as some remarkable breakthroughs. It was through tackling such difficult work that Ken was brought to realize that it is only the Holy Spirit of Christ within who can change age-old attitudes of suspicion and prejudice into strong attitudes of love, acceptance and forgiveness. However, the emotional strain of working for reconciliation in Belfast began to take its toll. Ken needed to discover deeper spiritual resources for his Christian life, and he started going to the regular clergy conferences held at the Christian Renewal Centre at Rostrevor, under the direction of the Rev Cecil Kerr. Slowly, through the ministry at Rostrevor and Ken's own prayers and reading, he came in 1979 into a new and refreshing experience of the power and life of the Holy Spirit.

Changes were taking place at Fitzroy Church and many new families started to attend. New songs were introduced to the worship and people gifted in being able to play the piano, drums, trumpet, viola and guitar were taking part. The members became concerned for the needs of the Third World, for overseas mission and door-to-door evangelism in the community.

In 1981, as a result of speaking on Radio Ulster's 'Thought for the Day', Ken came into contact with an old

Redemptorist priest in Clonard Monastery, Fr Christopher McCarthy. The priest had a deep love for the Scriptures and his vision was to found little Bible study groups where Catholics and Protestants could learn together. Since then there has come into being the Falls and Fitzroy Bible Study Fellowship in which between fifty and eighty Presbyterians and Catholics meet regularly for prayer and study of the Scriptures. Since the death of Fr McCarthy the Catholic side is being looked after by Fr Gerry Reynolds.

An important achievement in 1982 caught the attention of Irish newspapers all over the country. A sixty-three-year-old Catholic shopkeeper was murdered as he served behind his counter and on the day of the funeral Ken and some others arranged for forty-one Protestant clergymen to attend the service in a Catholic church. That number included four former moderators of the Presbyterian Church. They continued to attend the funerals of victims of violence, both Protestant and Catholic, for quite a while, to show a united conscience against all forms of violence. Such a united Protestant witness in a Catholic church had never been seen before. An editorial in the *Irish News* stated: 'We applaud their action and their words. We are confident they will receive broad support.'

In 1986 an event happened in Fitzroy which was the first such for almost 350 years. The Moderator of the Presbyterian Church in Ireland and the local Roman Catholic bishop spoke together on the theme 'There is hope in Christ' to an invited audience of nearly 400 Protestants and Catholics in Ken's church. Ken saw the service as though it were a candle shining in a dark night. It filled him with hope.

Ken is still very much a Christian Ulsterman with strong biblical beliefs. He would prefer to call himself British rather than Irish, but his desire is to be open to all people irrespective of their religious affiliation. He sees his own experience as like that of Saul of Tarsus before he met Christ. Once a narrow Jew, he met Christ, and was opened up to people of all nations.

Let Ken close this chapter by voicing his own present convictions: 'I believe that the Roman Catholic Church is a Christian church because its fundamental beliefs about Jesus Christ, his perfect life, atoning death, resurrection, ascension, and imminent return are identical with those described by Peter on the day of Pentecost. However there are certain areas of Catholic theology, such as the position of Mary, the nature of Christ's presence in the Eucharist, the influence of tradition, the belief in purgatory and the infallibility of the Pope, which need to be reformed in line with the original apostolic faith. Similar departures from that faith by Protestant churches also require reformation, such as the multiplicity of denominations that are clearly contrary to Scripture, the infrequent celebration of the Lord's Supper, the practice of indiscriminate baptism, the one-man ministry approach and the power of Protestant traditions rather than the word of God to shape the attitudes and practices of churches.

'There is a need for inter-church Bible studies as well as inter-church services. A new evaluation of Catholic theology is needed that is not emotionally aggressive or imbued with bitterness. As Protestants we have biblical insights to share with Catholics and they have insights that can enrich us.

'I find I cannot accept the doctrine of baptismal regeneration. I am glad that belief in transubstantiation and the nature of the eucharistic sacrifice is being examined afresh in the light of Scripture. I look forward to the day when Protestant and Catholic Christians can celebrate Communion together in a liturgy that is positively scriptural, such as the Lima liturgy. I rejoice that this has already begun to happen in a small way in some quarters.

'I am still essentially Reformed in my theology and would still sign the Westminster Confession of Faith, but that does not mean that every sentence of the Confession is binding on our consciences because only the word of God can have that status.'

So states a man who has slowly emerged from the influences of Ulster sectarianism. It has been a struggle and one that almost certainly would have taken much longer if it had not been for the years spent overseas in Holland and Indonesia, and also for the impact of friendships with other Christians.

8

An Untypical Priest

It is possible to be born into a Catholic family in Belfast, to be ordained into the priesthood and to live a normal, un-eventful but helpful and worth-while life as a priest. But things just did not work out that way for the Rev. Fr Hugh P. Murphy.

His story needs to be read alongside that of the Rev. Ken Newell in the previous chapter, to see how everyone born into either the Protestant or Catholic traditions in Northern Ireland has in some measure to try and break out of the binding influence of those moulds.

Although born in Belfast, Hugh Murphy's family moved to Holywood in the 1920s and in so doing moved into a Protestant environment. Holywood is a garrison town where British troops are stationed. Hugh and other Catholic children attended a church-run school and so grew up knowing few Protestants. Even when he moved to a grammar school it was one run by the church and so his friends continued to be mainly Catholic.

The greatest influence on his life in his early years was his home environment, and the faith of his parents and family. It was there that he began to see himself in the role of a priest and to sense God's call on his life. Even at seven years he would dress himself up in vestments with the aid of sheets of paper and pretend to say the Mass. No one questioned this decision, least of all himself, as it seemed so right. He went through Queen's University in Belfast, taking his BA in philosophy and Latin.

When the time came for theological training it was 1940, the Second World War was on and there was no possibility of going overseas so he joined some 600 students at the best known of all Irish theological colleges at Maynooth, Co. Kildare in the Republic. Four years of study took him through all the complexities of theology, patrology (studying the ancient Fathers of the church), canon law, church history, Greek, Hebrew, Old and New Testaments and much more besides.

While the countries of the world were blasting each other's cities to ruins and destroying the lives of tens of thousands, Hugh was a theological student preparing to spread the gospel. But in the year of D-Day, 1944, he had to face the world with all its complex hurts and problems and in a part of Ireland that had experienced the bombs and deaths. He was ordained as a diocesan priest by the Bishop of Down and Connor. It was the bishop's responsibility to decide where his first assignment should be. The most likely thing for any young priest to expect was to be posted as Curate to some parish with a parish priest to help him along the way. But right from the start Hugh was not to be a typical priest.

When Hitler's armies were sweeping across Europe it was likely that they would attack and capture the rock of Gibraltar in its crucial setting at the entrance to the Mediterranean Sea. In preparation for what in fact never happened the civilian population of Gibraltar was evacuated to London. With most Londoners in the forces there were plenty of jobs waiting to be filled, and the men from Gibraltar had no difficulty in earning good salaries. Then Germany began launching the deadly 'Doodlebug' flying bombs from across the channel on to the city of London. They caused the most terrible destruction and at first there seemed to be no answer to them. The Gibraltarians wanted to be taken out of the firing range to some safer territory. So it was that they were all shipped to Northern Ireland, to live in camps in various parts of the province. To Hugh Murphy's amazement he was called to the bishop's residence and asked to become chaplain to two of the camps in Co. Down.

With no practical experience of any kind behind him, he found himself surrounded by people of very mixed origin, descended from many nationalities, all calling themselves Roman Catholic and yet not interested in attending church. The local Irish people did not know what to make of them. It was their first confrontation with professing Catholics who did not practice their faith. Fr Hugh was similarly bemused in knowing how to bring such people into any meaningful experience of their faith. He wished he had a few years' experience of parish work behind him on which to call for ideas. He did not even have a church building—just the use of half a hut.

He was no longer isolated from the problems of the world. He was even starting to meet with Protestants, even visiting their homes for an occasional cup of tea—though avoiding the subjects of religion and politics.

Looking back he remembers his father's death in 1942 and how he noticed the local Church of Ireland rector in Holywood standing with hat raised in their street as the coffin passed. Such an event would pass unnoticed in most parts of the world, but in Northern Ireland it was a meeting of two faiths. That was as near as the two faiths could get to each other in many areas.

When a Protestant friend died Hugh can recall the experience of standing a distance from the open grave and away from the worshippers, so as not to associate himself with Protestant worship. Those were the days when it was a mortal sin to worship in a Protestant church. Most Catholics would have no conception at that time of what Protestants did or did not believe.

Looking over the shelves in a bookshop Hugh saw a volume on the life of Martin Luther. He took a quick look through its pages and realized that this was a very different man from the one about whom he had been taught. The great and unforgivable sin that Luther committed in the eyes of Catholic theologians was to get married. They did not blame him entirely for the Reformation. That was attributed more to King Henry VIII as a political manoeuvre to suit his own convenience.

This was all part of Hugh's background as he spent two years trying to serve Gibraltarians who needed the priest only for births, marriages and deaths. Hugh found it a dispiriting time. It was a relief to be moved to Donaghadee, along the east coast, where he spent eight years as Curate in charge of his own church while under the eyes of a parish priest at Newtownards.

Next door to Fr Hugh lived the Methodist minister, but in all those years the two men never spoke to each other. That saddens Hugh when he thinks of it now, but in those days there was no other known path to tread. He did, however, meet a Presbyterian layman, an outgoing person with a friendly manner, and the two men found it easy to strike up a relationship and have long talks together.

The next move was to Greencastle, near to the city of Belfast, where large housing estates were being built. Catholics were moving out of the troubled Falls Road area of Belfast, a ghetto area where never a Protestant would be seen, and they were going into the many rapidly expanding estates in Fr Hugh's parish. Conditions were vastly improved to those in the Falls Road but he soon discovered that the people were feeling very exposed, fearful and threatened. They were now meeting with Protestants, working alongside them, but not enjoying the experience. There was no hope of any socializing between the two sides. Catholics found themselves being called Fenians, a term they had not heard in the Falls Road.

After seven years in that curacy it began to look as

though Fr Hugh was at last finding the role that any typical priest would be expected to occupy—but then the bishop spoke again. This time he wanted Hugh to become a chaplain to the Royal Navy and to be accredited by the Admiralty in London. For the next twenty-five years he served as a commissioned chaplain in the Navy. Imagine this priest with such a slender association with Protestants walking into the officers' quarters of a Naval Reserve Unit in Belfast in the 1950s. There were seventy-two officers there and everyone of them a Protestant.

Many of those men belonged to the Orange Order. An unknown number were Freemasons. Fr Hugh was accepted because he had the right to be there and there was nothing anyone could do about it. He felt like a fish out of water. He was not even in to their heavy drinking habits.

When introductions were being made there was one captain who would always introduce Fr Hugh as their local IRA man. It was presumably meant as a joke, but underlying the remark was the belief that all Catholics were IRA sympathizers. He found it hurtful.

There were some killings by the IRA in the 1950s though nothing on the scale to take place in the following decade. Hugh preached against murder at one Mass and as a result was asked if he wanted police protection. He was amused at the idea, but in fact anyone who speaks out against men of violence can become one of their targets.

On another occasion a Dutch squadron of ships arrived at Belfast. That meant a complement of around 1,000 men, and 500 of those were Catholics. When he arranged a Mass for them about 450 attended. From that experience he learned that when Catholics and Protestants are evenly divided numerically they can learn to live together, which is something that has not been realized in Ireland, since one group or the other is always in minority.

A busy parish, a navy chaplain—and then came work with radio and television. He was arranging programmes, selecting speakers and doing broadcasts himself. His life was getting busier all the time. In 1960 he was transferred to St Mary's, a busy parish in the city of Belfast. Perhaps it was not all that surprising therefore that when he was in Portsmouth on naval business he suffered three coronaries and was nursed at the naval hospital.

After a time of convalescence on the Isle of Wight he was back in Belfast in full fling again, taking on duties with the Samaritans and running a religious bookshop in Belfast. The bishop wisely transferred him to rest at Portrush, on the northern coastline, but he felt isolated and lost there. After five years he became a parish priest at Ahoghill, just outside Ballymena, a Protestant area with a strong Orange Order membership. It was here that the first of two dramatic incidents took place in his life.

As a member of the British Legion he was asked to conduct the Remembrance Day service at the war memorial in Ballymena in 1977. The members of the Legion were glad to find a fellow member who was also a clergyman to lead in the service. The Rev. Ian Paisley, along with the members of the Free Presbyterian Church and some others, objected to a Catholic priest conducting the service. They put pressure on the organizers to cancel the arrangement, but the British Legion stood firm by their decision. Dr Paisley then ordered his followers to boycott the service, and he then went ahead with plans to have their own service of remembrance immediately after the official one.

Instead of Irish people being able to unite in honouring those who died in two world wars, the Catholic-Protestant issue had once again caused a split. They were unable to stand together even round a war memorial. The incident caught the attention of the world's press and was featured with headlines in both British and Irish newspapers. As Fr Hugh and the others officiating in the service walked to the platform they were met by a battery of cameramen. He wore the robes of a Navy chaplain and was careful to include in his prayers an intercession for the Queen— something that the 'loyalist' service apparently omitted to do. There were 2,500 people at the service and as soon as it was over the next procession arrived, some 1,000 people, for a service conducted by a minister of the Independent Methodist Church.

Being ecumenical in Ahoghill was never easy, although Fr Hugh had discovered that even before the Remembrance Day service took place. When he first arrived he set out at the beginning of January to visit all the other ministers to wish them a happy new year. He was received politely, but no one ever returned the call. When the next year came round he realized that he might only be embarrassing the other men, so he never did it again.

On another occasion he was invited to speak to the young people at a Presbyterian church in Belfast on the Second Vatican Council, the one at which Pope John had started to make revolutionary changes within the Roman Catholic Church. The Free Presbyterians and Ian Paisley heard about this and voiced their objections to a Catholic priest speaking on Presbyterian premises. They threatened to send twenty-three bus loads of protestors to the church when the meeting was on. So far as Fr Hugh was concerned he was prepared to go ahead no matter what happened, but he realized how difficult the situation had become for the Presbyterian minister so he offered to withdraw from the meeting. As a result the meeting was cancelled and of course Ian Paisley and his followers claimed this as a moral victory for themselves.

Then came 18th June 1978, a date that Fr Hugh will never forget. It was the anniversary of his ordination and at 7 a.m. on that Sunday he heard the front door bell ringing. He looked out of the window and saw a man standing with his face so close to the door that it was not possible to make out his features. Fr Hugh called to the man and asked what was wrong. The man replied that the priest was needed urgently. The fact that the man never stood back from the door, or looked up to the window, made Fr Hugh think that he must be drunk. He slipped on his dressing gown and went down to open the door. As he did he was confronted by a man with a mask over his face and a gun in his hand. It appeared to be the same man and he repeated that the priest was needed urgently.

The only conclusion Fr Hugh could come to was that the man was a member of the IRA, that a colleague of his had been shot and wanted to receive the last rites of the Church.

A second man appeared and, forcing his arms behind his back, they rushed him down the steps. Fr Hugh said that he did not have the holy oil with him and he would need that, but this did not seem to register with the men. That made him start to think that perhaps they were not Catholics. They said they were from the Irish Republican Army but he doubted the truth of that. When his glasses fell off they left them on the ground, saying he would not need them.

As they approached a car his hands were tied behind his back and a blindfold placed over his eyes. One man commented: 'I hope you don't have a heart problem.' Fr Hugh said that he did, as they bundled him into the back of a car. Fr Hugh knew all the roads well in that area. He hoped to be able to follow the route they took by the turns the car made. He was quick to notice that when the man beside him said, 'Turn right,' the car turned left. This procedure was followed through the journey; what they were doing was taking a circuitous route so as to end up only half-a-mile from Fr Hugh's front door.

As he was taken from the car, still blindfolded, the man told him to get the feel of cold steel and pressed the barrel of the gun into his forehead. Fr Hugh tried some humour by saying that it did not feel very cold to him, but it did not get any response. He was taken into a disused barn. Throughout his captivity only the one man ever spoke to him.

It was he who unfolded the true story. The IRA had attacked two policemen, killing one and abducting the other. There were fears that the captured policeman might be undergoing torture and it was for this reason that the priest was captured. It was hoped that the Roman Catholic

Cardinal in Ireland might appeal to the IRA to release the policeman in order to save the life of the priest. It was made clear to Fr Hugh that if the policeman was not released that day they would 'squash him like a fly'. He was convinced in his own mind that he would be going to meet the Lord some time that day.

It eventually transpired that the man who did the talking was in fact a policeman who was taking the law into his own hands to try and save the life of his colleague.

There was nothing Hugh could do except pray and he devoted himself to this in every moment he had. It was a terrifying experience, knowing what gunmen had done and were doing in Ireland in those days.

News of his capture and of the threats being made on his life were being broadcast almost constantly on a local radio station. Fr Hugh could hear helicopters overhead as they searched for suspicious movements on the ground. They provided his only hope of being rescued.

What no one had realized was that the missing policeman, believed captured, was already dead. His body was kept in water for three days, the killers waiting for the heat to die down before allowing his body to be found.

Then the almost impossible happened. Ian Paisley was a strict keeper of the Sabbath and would never do a broadcast on a Sunday. On this Sunday he went on the local radio station and appealed for the release of the priest.

Ian Paisley is an enigma to many people. They see his actions as constantly contradicting each other, preaching a gospel of peace and threatening war and strife. There is no incongruity in Paisley's mind, and his action to save the life of a priest was quite consistent to his thinking.

Fr Hugh knew he was in the hands of militant Protestants who looked on Paisley as their pope, king and everything else rolled into one. He did not, however, know about Paisley's broadcast. In his thinking there was no hope of the IRA releasing a policeman unharmed, so therefore his own death was certain. He thought his fear was to be confirmed that evening when he heard a car driving up to the barn, and his blindfold was removed and a coal sack was pulled down over his head and shoulders. He was walked outside and told to lie down in the back of a station wagon. It seemed obvious to Fr Hugh that he would be driven to some lonely country lane, taken out of the vehicle and shot dead—his body left at the roadside.

He made one last desperate attempt to save his life by asking the gunman if he might talk to him. If a conversation could be started there was at least a hope that he could talk his way to freedom. But the request was refused, the gunman saying that Fr Hugh was going to be released. He did not believe that for a moment. It sounded like a ruse to keep him quiet.

They drove away, leaving him with his only standby: to keep on praying. When the car stopped and he was pulled out he was convinced his last moment had come. Instead the car drove away and he was left standing at the roadside. He struggled with the coal sack and managed to shake it from his head. He could see the station wagon disappearing down the road so he started to walk in the opposite direction.

He was looking for a house with a telephone line attached to it. He couldn't see any lines, but he decided to approach the next house he saw anyway. As he walked up the driveway he saw faces at a window and then they disappeared. Nearing the doorway he spotted someone looking round the side of the house and then moving away. It made him very apprehensive about how he was going to be received. He had not realized it at the time, but his face was black from the coal sack, and he looked a very strange sight walking up the driveway in pyjamas and dressing gown! Then he heard his name being called and quickly realized he was at the home of one of his parishioners. There were tears of relief and joy all round as he was greeted and taken inside.

He tried to ring his home but could not get through, so he dialled 999 and spoke to the police. After they phoned him back to confirm that it was a genuine call and not a trap, he was soon in a police car on his way to the station to make a statement. He could hear the police speaking over the car radio in code. They were saying: 'We have the parcel, everything is all right.'

Even the scene in the police station was an emotional one, but it was nothing compared to his arrival back home. The house was full of neighbours and friends, including local clergy, Catholic and Protestant. In the next few weeks letters of joy celebrating his escape came to him from all over the world.

In four weeks he was moved to Coleraine, to what it was hoped would be safer territory. In six months the police caught the kidnapper and he was sent to prison.

Fr Hugh phoned Ian Paisley to thank him and also expressed his thanks publicly on television, stating that he supposed he would now have to vote for Paisley. When the missing policemen's body was found and the funeral service took place, Fr Hugh went along. He found it a very moving experience to be there, mourning a death that could so easily have brought about his own killing. Paisley was there too and the two men shook hands.

Since that experience Fr Hugh has had great feeling for all people held hostage. He has made a point of publicly befriending the police since realizing the constant danger in which they live. Frequently he has publicly praised them for their work as a means of showing his forgiveness for their few erring members. Looking back to that incident, Fr Hugh believes that he would find it very difficult to meet the man who held him captive. That man saw into Fr Hugh's very bones, saw his fear and all that he went through that day. Such a meeting could be embarrassing for them both, but having talked with Fr Hugh I cannot see him ever refusing to meet the man.

There were two specific prayers that he prayed while in captivity, and he believes that the Lord answered them both. The first was that he would remain calm. The second was that he would have the courage to face whatever lay in front of him. He experienced both of these in deep measure.

Now he is in a small parish of about 100 families at Whitehouse, north of Belfast. His main life's work is to build up ecumenical relations. His sits on numerous committees and sometimes feels he is planning endless services that no one wants to attend, but he does not give up. He gets good support from the Catholic community who can see the value of what he is attempting to do. He encourages people to speak positively about every situation, as he believes that negative talk is doing great harm in the province.

In the Catholic Church the retirement age for a priest is seventy-five. He is happy to continue his present ecumenical stand until then, or even beyond that age. The opposition he faces is still very strong, but he holds on to the flashes of humour that shine through it all. On one occasion an ecumenical service was announced where the Protestant speaker was to speak first, followed by a Catholic priest, himself. For some reason the order was changed at the last moment so he spoke first. The protestors in the congregation listened to him quite happily, thinking he was the Protestant minister. When the Protestant entered the pulpit he was heckled as a Catholic who should not be in a Protestant pulpit.

Fr Hugh Murphy has not lived the life of a typical priest, but he has shown the price that may have to be paid in Northern Ireland if a priest starts reaching out to accept the Protestant community. Not everyone is prepared to pay that price.

9
She Loved Much

Her many sins have been forgiven—for she loved much. But he who has been forgiven little loves little (Luke 7:47).

To understand correctly the link between forgiveness and love it is vital to interpret this saying of Jesus as he meant it. It must be seen in the context of the whole story he was telling. If the two sentences quoted are lifted out of their context and seen on their own, the suggestion is that the woman in the story loved Jesus greatly and therefore her many sins were forgiven. In that case love would come first and then forgiveness.

From the context of the whole story in Luke 7:35–50 it is clear that Jesus was teaching that God's forgiveness comes first and is followed by our grateful love to him. The greater the forgiveness we have experienced the greater will be our response of love.

A few Bible translators have tried to ensure that the correct meaning is taken. The Jerusalem Bible, first published in English in 1966, gets it right: 'Her sins, her many sins, must have been forgiven her, or she would not have shown such great love. It is the man who is forgiven little who shows little love.' The New English Bible also tries to get it right: 'Her great love proves that her many sins have

111

been forgiven; where little has been forgiven, little love is shown.' It is a pity that the New International Version and other modern translations do not make the meaning equally clear.

Let us understand this truth then—God does not forgive us because we love him. We love God because he forgave us.

We also need to understand what Jesus meant when he spoke of a man having few sins forgiven. Jesus was not suggesting that the man in the story had not committed many sins and so did not need a great deal of forgiveness in order to have them covered. The man in the story, Simon the Pharisee, who invited Jesus to his home for a meal, was so full of self-righteous pride that he was not aware of the many sins in his life. He thought of himself as far superior to the woman whose sins were known all over the town. Because he was blind to his sinfulness he had confessed very few sins to God and so had experienced very little in the way of forgiveness from God. The sad result was that Simon had little love for God, and none for Jesus.

Right through the story Simon refers to the woman as a sinner but never sees himself in that category. He is incapable of showing any forgiveness to the woman.

An important principle is emerging here. If I am going to be capable of forgiving the people who have hurt me most deeply, I must be aware of the extent to which I have been forgiven by God. The great danger is that I will consider the person who has hurt me to be a greater sinner than I am: 'I have never hurt anyone in *that* way,' or '*I* would never commit such a dreadful sin.' By allowing myself to think along those lines I am moving into the sin of pride and self-righteousness. I am ignoring the fact that in God's eyes we are all equal. We are all sinners. God does not classify people into big sinners and little sinners. He calls on us to repent for being sinners, not just for the sins we have committed. My sinfulness puts me on a par with all other sinners. We are not judged by the number of sins we have committed. We are judged because we are sinners.

When I get this thinking right, then I realize that God needed as much forgiveness to meet my need as he does for the person I am unable to forgive. It is only as I realize how much I have been forgiven, and that it took the death of Jesus to achieve that forgiveness, that I have a great love for God, and out of that love I am able to forgive everyone who sins against me.

Now let us look at some other aspects of this story. When Jesus said to the woman: 'Your sins are forgiven' (verse 48), he was not forgiving her at that moment. He was proclaiming her forgiveness, assuring her of the forgiveness she had received some time previously. When Jesus said in verse 47, 'Her many sins have been forgiven,' he was speaking in the past tense, referring to a forgiveness that had taken place previously. This explains the great love that the woman had for Jesus, the tears of gratitude she wept, the kisses she gave, the perfume with which she anointed him.

I can picture her standing in a crowd of people some days previously, listening to Jesus preach. She heard him speak of repentance and forgiveness and in that moment she repented of her sinful nature and God's forgiveness flooded through her life. She had never experienced anything like it. All she had ever known was the condemnation of the world that saw her as a public sinner. Now she was overwhelmed with love for the One who had brought forgiveness to her.

She waited for an opportunity to express her gratitude and it came in Simon's house. When a feast was held in Israel the front door was always left open so that anyone might walk in, though uninvited guests would merely be spectators of the meal. She would have no trouble walking in and standing at the feet of Jesus.

Everything she did from then on showed her gratitude for Jesus and her love for him, but in Simon's eyes she was always a sinner and he could find no forgiveness in his heart.

The fact that Jesus received the woman's gratitude and

love shows that he knew all about her and knew the repentance that had taken place. Simon said of Jesus: 'If this man were a prophet, he would know who is touching him and what kind of woman she is—that she is a sinner' (verse 39). In fact it was Simon who failed to see what kind of woman she was—repentant and forgiven.

This leads us to the principle that we must never withhold forgiveness from someone whom God has forgiven. We must go even further than that. If the person has not yet repented of his sin, we must hold out forgiveness to him because that is what God is doing, and what God has done to us.

We are not told how Simon reacted to what Jesus said. I think the reason for this is so that we can put ourselves in Simon's place and decide what our response would be. Would we find it in our hearts to forgive as Jesus forgives, or would we continue to refer to the repentant woman as a sinner and see ourselves as more righteous than her?

Simon was not in the forgiving business. He was more at home in the business of condemnation, and it was not just the woman he was condemning. Her visit to his home was an unexpected one, but the visit of Jesus had been carefully arranged. I believe Simon had planned to condemn Jesus as a false prophet and to do it publicly in front of all his invited guests. From the moment Jesus arrived at the house Simon snubbed him in front of the guests, denying Jesus all the customary Eastern courtesies of water with which to wash his feet, a kiss of welcome on the hand or cheek. This behaviour would have shocked the watching guests for it was the height of rudeness, and it would have shown them immediately that a conflict had been opened up between the two men, Simon and Jesus. All eyes would be fixed on them to see which would win.

When a visiting rabbi or any kind of teacher was in town it was usual for some person of standing to open their home, lay on a meal and have an evening's intellectual discussion. All would share their reaction to the teacher's particular theme and the talk could continue late into the night. The last thing the host would want would be the intrusion of an emotional woman who could not control her feelings and who was more interested in her personal experience than intellectual debate.

Simon also had a problem in that he knew the woman's sinful reputation, and as a Pharisee he was bound by law to keep himself pure from such company. If he so much as touched the woman, or let her touch him, he would be unclean and would have to go through a complete process of purification before he could mix with people again. This explains his horror at the way in which Jesus, a so-called prophet of God, allowed the woman to touch him without making any effort to escape from her.

The fact that the guests were reclining on couches around the food denotes that it was a formal occasion, a banquet. The normal procedure would be for basins to be placed under the feet of each guest as they lay full length, leaning on one arm, and for servants to pour refreshing water over the feet. This was not done for Jesus until the woman poured her tears of gratitude over his feet. Those tears were spontaneous, uncontrolled and as they fell she was embarrassed and wanted to wipe the feet dry, but she had no cloth. Quickly she let down her hair and used the long tresses as a towel. A gasp must have gone up from the guests, for in the East no woman would let down her hair in public. Only the husband would ever see his wife with her hair down. What amazed everyone present was the way in which Jesus reacted. He took no steps to stop what the woman was doing, to reprimand her or to move away. He accepted everything she did as though there was something wonderfully right about it all.

Simon's role as a Pharisee should have been to welcome a repentant sinner back into the fellowship of believers at the synagogue and at the temple. Every repentant sinner needs the close fellowship and understanding of fellow believers, but if a church is not able to forgive then its doors will be closed to such people. What is even worse, the hearts of the people will be closed. Simon could not recognize the repentance that was evident in the tears. He could not understand the acceptance that Christ manifested to the woman. When he looked at the woman all he could see was the sin of her past, not the beauty of her present forgiveness.

This incident in the life of Christ is showing us that forgiveness is not an optional commodity. It is absolutely essential for every Christian. We need to accept how great has been our sinfulness, how glorious is God's forgiveness, and to let our hearts overflow with love for God because we have been forgiven so much. Then, and only then, will we be able to forgive others and to receive them with warm loving hearts into full Christian fellowship.

However, it is not Simon who grips my attention in this report. I am sorry for him that his heart could remain so cold and hard, but my eyes are transfixed by the picture of Jesus lying full length, his head resting on one arm and the woman pouring out her tears on his feet and breaking open her jar of perfume to anoint him with its sweetness. The story reads as though she had bought the perfume specially for this purpose. The normal procedure would have been to anoint the head with oil. Jesus said to Simon: 'You did not put oil on my head' (verse 46). The woman did not feel worthy to approach the head of Jesus. She felt more at home by his feet and so she poured the perfume over his feet. The anointing was the same and Jesus received it as a further expression of the woman's love.

Although the woman did not intend it that way, it seems to me that everything she did was a condemnation of the Pharisee. She was doing for Jesus all the things that he had deliberately neglected to do. His aim was to insult his guest. Her aim was to love her Saviour.

The first and greatest commandment is to love God, and this is something that every Christian desires to do, but we see from this incident that our ability to love God is dependent upon the degree to which we have acknowledged that we are all equally sinners in God's sight, all equally in need of forgiveness, all equally dependent upon his grace. Our love for God will always be a response to his love for us in forgiving all our sins. If we love little perhaps we have never acknowledged the degree of our own sinfulness and therefore the greatness of God's forgiveness.

10

Father's Initiative

In the last chapter we saw that our love for God is a response to his love for us in forgiving us all our sins. Now we need to spend a while looking at that love when it is manifested towards a sinner. It was the Father's love that set the whole plan of salvation in motion. He sent his only Son into the world to become our Saviour. The Father took the initiative in providing for man's salvation.

This love is exemplified in the parable Jesus told of the lost son, following his stories of the lost coin and the lost sheep. It is usually called the parable of the prodigal son (Luke 15:11–32), and is recorded only by Luke, but for our purpose we want to look at the story from the father's perspective.

The first fact to note in relation to the father is that his property would never normally have been divided among his sons until after his death. In the Middle East no child would ever think of asking for his inheritance while his father was still alive. This is shown in Hebrews 9:16–17: 'A will is in force only when somebody has died; it never takes effect while the one who made it is living.'

For the youngest son in this story to ask for his inheritance while his father was alive can mean only one thing—the relationship between him and his father had got so bad that he wished his father was dead. He was not prepared to look after his father and care for him in his old age. He wanted his father dead now. He wanted his inheritance immediately.

The father's natural reaction would be to refuse any such request, to reprimand his son and to order him back to his work in the fields. That is what the local community would expect the father to do. It would therefore have been almost unbelievable when the father raised not the slightest objection to the request, offered no criticism of his son, but gave him everything for which he asked.

This story runs parallel to our own experience. The sin in my life puts me in a completely wrong relationship with my Father in heaven. I cannot think straight about things that are holy and pure. I am living in rebellion against God, and yet I start demanding my inheritance in heaven, the right to live there. The Father has every right to reject my request, to order me out of his presence, but so great is his love that he offers no word of criticism but agrees to my request— even if it means the death of his Son Jesus to make it possible for me to receive my inheritance.

The next thing to note about the father in the story is that when he divided up his property he gave both his sons their share. The eldest son received his inheritance also. This meant that the father had now lost all his possessions and had to live the rest of his life completely dependent upon his sons to feed and clothe him. The reaction of the eldest son should have been to refuse to accept his inheritance, to insist on waiting for his father's death before inheriting, to devote his life to looking after his father's property rather than taking it from him.

When the eldest son accepted his inheritance it could only mean that he also wished that his father was dead. This shows just how bad relationships had become in that family. But again the father had no criticism of either son. He accepted them just as they were, with all their wrong attitudes and all their greed.

Acceptance of people and of situations has to be present

before we can love them. This is what Paul had in mind when he wrote: 'Accept one another, then, just as Christ accepted you, in order to bring praise to God' (Romans 15:7). Christ does not say to the rebellious sinner, 'Change your way of life and cease your rebellious spirit and then I will accept you.' He accepts us exactly as we are, with all our rebellion, and once he has accepted us he is able to love us, and it is his love that brings forth our response, the change in our lives. Do not try to love people if you have not first accepted them just as they are, with all their faults.

Psalm 133:1 states: 'How good and pleasant it is when brothers live together in unity!' The two brothers in the parable were united in sin and rebellion and there is nothing good or pleasant about that kind of unity.

It appears that the younger son quickly sold his share of the property. He was going into a far country and the land would be no good to him there. He wanted money to spend on a life of luxury and high living. When he began selling what should have been his father's property the local community would have been horrified at such disrespect for the father. They would have treated the son with utter contempt. Family life was a sacred thing among the Israelites and a community consisted of families closely knit together, not like this family.

To add to his disgrace in the eyes of the local people at home it would appear that he spent all his money in a Gentile country. When famine came and he had to look for work he was obviously employed by a Gentile to look after pigs—animals considered unclean by Jews and therefore never kept by them. He had really reached rock bottom to undertake such work, and to serve a Gentile would mean he would not be able to observe the Sabbath. His religious observance had been frittered away by his sin.

The pods fed to the pigs would not be the rich nourishing kind that were sweet to the taste and full of energy. They were too precious a commodity, in time of famine, to feed the pigs. Instead they would be the wild kind, bitter to the taste and with little nourishment in them. When the son ate them they failed to satisfy his hunger.

The fact that 'No one gave him anything' (verse 16) could suggest that he resorted to begging to try and ease his plight, but without success.

Then we see him back with his father and their moment of meeting needs to be clearly understood. The father would have known that if his son ever returned the whole village would turn against him for the way he had treated his father and broken up the home. The son would be surrounded by jeering, scoffing crowds who might easily resort to physical attack. Perhaps it was to prevent this happening that the father took the initiative and ran to meet his son as soon as he appeared in sight. The father spoke not a word of condemnation or rebuke but greeted his son with the kiss of reconciliation, complete acceptance and forgiveness.

This would have astounded the villagers. There was no way they could ridicule the son when he had been accepted by the very person he had hurt and insulted. The father saved the son from people's condemnation by his complete acceptance. The lad had a carefully prepared speech ready, but it did not come out as he had intended. His father's love and forgiveness immediately brought about a change in his life. He had intended demanding that he be taken on as a hired servant, paid a wage so that he could live independently in the village, not dependent upon his brother in any way. He would rather be humiliated by the villagers than have to live with his brother. But when he did make his speech to his father he didn't get as far as the bit about being a hired servant. Instead his speech was one of repentance, humility and reconciliation. He was back in the family relationship, united with his father again, and the only thing left to do now was to rejoice and celebrate.

The fact that a calf was killed for the meal shows that the whole village was being invited to celebrate. It would provide too much food for any smaller gathering. The playing of music, that the elder son heard, was the signal that the meal was ready and everyone was to come. As the people arrived they would see the son wearing his father's best robe, a further indication of the reconciliation that had taken place.

The Father in heaven is seen in every detail of this reconciliation, even to the fact that we are clothed in his righteousness. The marriage feast of the Lamb is prepared for us and there is no condemnation for those who are in Christ Jesus (Romans 8:1).

Now watch the father's attitude to the elder son who hears the music on his way in from the fields. His journey home was proving as difficult as his brother's had been. Once the elder son discovered that all the village was assembling for a feast given by his father, he would have known that there were certain duties that the villagers would expect him to perform. As the elder son it would be expected that he would circulate among the guests—greeting them, showing his complete acceptance of his father's celebration and giving a special embrace to the honoured guest, in this case his younger brother.

The assembled guests would have been horrified to find that the elder son was not present to perform his duties, especially if they heard his angry outburst in refusing to go in. They would all have expected the father to go out in a rage, confront the son and publicly reprimand him, but instead they saw the father going to the son, accepting him without a word of rebuke and actually entreating him to come in to the feast and enjoy himself. The father offered equal reconciliation to both sons.

The law of Moses said that a rebellious son was to be stoned to death by the men of the village (Deuteronomy 21:18–21). All the men would have been ready to put this law into effect, but they were forestalled by the father's acceptance, love and forgiveness.

How the elder son responded is left in the air. The story ends without that being revealed. In telling the story Jesus wanted his listeners, once again, to put themselves in the place of the elder son and to decide how they would react to such an offer of forgiveness, especially when they saw the younger son's response.

Forgiveness when given publicly is a costly act that may be misunderstood by the onlookers. God, the heavenly Father, offered his complete forgiveness in a very public way at Calvary. How each individual will respond is left as an open question, for no one person can respond for someone else.

We are not told how long it took the younger son to spend all his money, how long he was away from his father, but it might well have been some years. The real healing needed was for that original moment of rebellion when he demanded his inheritance, so it was an event of the past for which forgiveness had to come. We are now going to look at an up-to-date example of forgiveness being needed for an event long since past.

11

Torpedoed in Wartime

It was not the most successful wartime journey for HMS Asturias in July 1943. This large and rather cumbersome armed merchant cruiser gave a great feeling of security to the small merchant ships travelling in convoy across the Atlantic. It looked so big and strong, 22,000 tons of solid metal blasting a path through the waves with eight six-inch guns pointing menacingly towards the horizon, ready to take on any German or Italian warships that dared to threaten any of the ships under its protection.

The smaller, sleek frigates that scurried round the edges of the convoys, hurrying on the stragglers and setting the pace for them all, were an important part of the security screen for the precious cargo of food and supplies that crossed from America to Britain, but they never looked as sure a defence as the massive cruiser. The sheer size of the big ship made it more of a psychological weapon than anything else. In fact she was very vulnerable to submarines and not capable of fast evasive action against either torpedoes or attacks from the air.

The young cadet from Northern Ireland, David McConnell, who formed a small part of the crew of 300 men, had his own feeling of security on such a big ship. He was enjoying the busy life and the comradeship that is a special part of the life of every naval crew. It was proving to be an eventful journey. They had started from Brazil, providing part of the escort for a large dry dock that was being towed by ocean tugs to West Africa.

In the South Atlantic they experienced the heavy seas that only that part of the world can produce. About half way through their long journey the constant pounding of the huge waves proved too much for a dock that was constructed for calmer waters, and it began to break up. There was nothing that could be done to save it. The mission had to be written off as another victory for the seas over even the strongest of man-made structures. This was no new experience for sailors who quickly learn to respect the powers of nature and never to underestimate the force behind even one Atlantic wave. The escort vessels sailed off on their own for Africa, the frigates and corvettes keeping an eye on the slower Asturias but keen to reach port as soon as possible.

Unknown to any of them there was another eye watching the big ship, from the periscope of an Italian submarine gliding as quietly as possibly beneath the ocean swells. The captain was a young man who sensed that the end of the war was near and that there was no hope of a victory for Italy. Whatever happened to Germany and the Allies it looked as though Italy would come out the loser in any event. The Italian captain already had it in mind to surrender his ship and crew to the Allies and get out of the conflict, as many other ships were doing, but just at this moment he had a rich prize in his sights. It would be good to go out of the war with such a personal victory under his belt.

The best target was undoubtedly the largest ship in the convoy, the Asturias, but the captain was very conscious of the smaller and much faster ships that surrounded it. If any one of them picked up the noise of his engines on their sonar equipment every ship would be dropping depth charges and his hope of survival would be nil. As he viewed the scene there was no sign that anyone had detected his presence. There was complete silence among his crew. The adrenalin was flowing fast through their veins. They were all feeling that strange mixture of fear and excitement that sets the heart pounding faster.

There was always the risk of his torpedo missing one of the smaller, faster vessels, but on the other hand there was a better chance of escaping if he aimed at a ship on the outskirts of the convoy. He took another look at the scene, made up his mind and lowered the periscope. He had decided on the most dangerous plan of all, to sail underneath the smaller ships and surface inside the convoy, aiming his torpedo at the cruiser and then hoping by some unimaginable piece of good fortune to get back outside the convoy again. It seemed an impossible risk to take. If he scored a hit the sound of the explosion would be heard all over the convoy and every ship would turn on him. It was a tremendous risk to take, but the prize of the big ship seemed too good to miss.

The submarine submerged and glided underneath the escort vessels. The engines, smooth and gentle, sounded like the pounding of thunder to the crew. It seemed impossible that the noise would not be picked up by one of the ships. When they raised periscope again the convoy was still sailing on its course, oblivious to the presence of the enemy in their midst. And there in front of them was the prize, the large hull of the cruiser, a prime target for any experienced submarine commander.

The order was given to fire and a torpedo began to slice its way through the waters, straight for its target. The submarine submerged quickly to slip away, every ear strained for the sound of an explosion on the surface. Then it came. A direct hit amidships that crippled the cruiser, breaking its back, silencing its engines, cutting off all power and light and causing the bow and stern to rise out of the waters heavenwards. She stood there poised to sink to the depths at a moment's notice.

David McConnell will never forget the sound of that explosion. The sound tore through him as savagely as the torpedo tore a hole in the ship's hull. Nearly forty-five years later when I sat with David in his beautiful Thames-side home in Twickenham, London, he could still remember that frightening sound and feel the impact in his bones.

Four men died. The rest of the crew rushed to the decks to their emergency stations beside lifeboats and rafts, waiting for the order to abandon ship. It never came. The ship lay where it was hit, lifeless, unable to move and, for some strange reason, unable to sink.

Every man held his breath, almost afraid to take a step or make a move in case they precipitated the vessel's plunge to the depths. The captain of the cruiser had the lives of 300 men in his hands. He could order them to the boats to be picked up by their escort vessels or he could wait to see if the stubborn old ship would stay afloat. If it sank quickly the men might not all have time to escape.

Then he realized that the escort vessels had disappeared into the darkness, unaware of the presence of the submarine and not even hearing the sound of the explosion. The Italian captain and crew could not believe their ears. All noise of enemy engines had faded into the distance. It sounded as though they had the ocean to themselves. They kept sailing until they reached the security of the port at Durban in South Africa where the captain surrendered his ship and, so far as he and his crew were concerned, ended the war.

Back on board the crippled Asturias the crew spent each night lying on the decks, afraid to go below in case the ship sank, unable to shine a torch in case they attracted the submarine back to take a second shot. It was the 25th July when the attack took place and the ship wallowed helplessly in the heavy seas for over a week. They had sent out a distress signal stating that they had been hit and this was relayed round the world to London and from there back to one of the escort vessels. This was the first indication the escort received that anything was wrong. One of them turned and sped back to the stricken cruiser. It laid a smoke screen round the ship to obscure her from view, ensured she was not sinking and then sped away again.

David McConnell remembers those days and nights very well. It seemed like an eternity, everyone tense and in a constant state of anticipation for the moment when the ship would sink, taking them with it. It left a scar on each man's memory that time would not erase. They talked together about the attack, the submarine and its commander. There was general agreement that the man was incredibly brave to have risked sailing underneath the escort ships. Many must have felt feelings of bitterness and resentment at the way in which they had been left, stranded in such a helpless and almost suicidal situation.

At long last a tug arrived, took them in tow and hauled them to Freetown in West Africa where the crew walked to safety, leaving behind the sad spectacle of their ship lying helpless and unwanted. David was sent home to England.

After several jobs, at which he worked very hard, he finally retired at the age of sixty, in 1983, apart from some part-time consultancy work.

With more time on his hands he began devoting himself increasingly to Christian work. He and his wife are very committed to the local Church of England that they attend, but he is also very active with Gideons International, a movement for placing copies of the Bible in hotels, schools, hospitals and prisons. In 1980 a new branch of Gideons was started in central London where there are 600,000 people and the challenge of providing Scriptures in 600 hotels, twenty-four schools, fourteen hospitals, and one large prison. There are six men in the branch involved in the distribution work and in their first six years they placed 70,000 copies of the Scriptures where they are most likely to be read.

In the midst of this busy life, extending over forty-four years since his ship was torpedoed and wrecked, David has never been able to forget the shock of the explosion and the trauma of those days and nights spent clinging to the deck of that stricken vessel. The experience was still real to him. He felt for all his friends who had suffered alongside him and for the men who had died. He knew that somewhere in Italy or elsewhere in the world there lived the man who had captained that submarine, who had selected his target and ordered the torpedo to be fired.

David knew that the incident was long since buried in history, but that did not stop it from being very much alive in his mind. He felt a growing desire to try and trace the Italian captain and put things right between them. In nautical terms it would be like 'clearing the decks', wiping clean the memory of the event so as to make sure that there was no resentment left in his heart.

In February, 1986 he wrote to the Italian embassy asking if there was any possibility of tracing the identity of the submarine and the name and whereabouts of the captain. He enclosed details of the wartime attack.

The embassy passed on the enquiry to the Historical Branch of the Italian Navy and the requested information came through later that same month. He was sent the complete history of the submarine together with a photograph of the vessel. At the time of the attack it was captained by Guiseppi Roselli Lorenzini, and his career was listed from 1929 to 1973. To David's surprise he found that the man who surrendered his ship at Durban went on in his naval career to become Chief of Staff in the Italian Navy and, later still, an admiral with NATO (North Atlantic Treaty Organisation).

The most important news of all was that the admiral was alive. David wrote him a long letter introducing himself, reminding the admiral of the attack at sea, but assuring him that if the two of them could now be fully reconciled to each other over the years, the incident could be put behind them and so far as David was concerned would be past and gone for ever. He offered complete forgiveness for the suffering and death caused to his friends. He also assured him that he and the rest of the British crew had all remarked on the courage of the Italian captain in taking the risk of sailing underneath the escort ships.

At long last, in September 1986, David received a reply from the Italian admiral, then retired. It came from Rome and in the letter he explained how he had kept in touch over the years with all the surviving crew of the submarine. He had made copies of David's letter and sent it to each crew member so that they too could become part of the reconciliation. He wrote: 'They very much appreciated your sportsmanship.'

A widow of one of the Italian crew, living in Bologna, also wrote to him when she received a copy of his letter. She explained that her husband had died that September, just before the letter arrived, and so had not received it. She thanked David for writing.

In David's sitting room I saw a framed photograph of Asturias and attached to it a picture of the submarine and a portrait of the distinguished looking admiral in full uniform. He also has a picture of the same man when he was captain of the submarine, taken on the conning tower.

'I had to make that contact,' David told me. 'The incident had niggled me for years. I knew that there could not be forgiveness until I had expressed it to the captain.'

David wrote again sending an Italian translation of the New Testament to the admiral. In his reply expressing thanks for this gift the admiral stated that 'this marvellous little book is now my bed book'. David has a mental picture of this one-time enemy now united with him through the act of forgiveness and their common love for God's word.

David is still very much part of Ireland and of its problems. He has a niece living in Canada whose husband left Ireland when his life was threatened by the IRA because he identified men who had been involved in a raid on a bank.

'Christ is the only way for Ireland. In mathematics you

must have a common denominator. Christ is that common denominator who can bring both sides together,' he told me.

As I listened to David I realized how well he illustrated the truth that forgiveness in God's sight must involve the putting away of the sin out of our minds. This is what God meant in his promise, 'I will remember their sins no more.' That needs to be looked at in greater detail, so it is the theme of the next chapter. David's memory carried the hurts of his experience for over forty years, and he was not happy until he had wiped his mind clean of those hurts through the act of forgiveness.

12

Remember No More

When the Lord makes a promise in the Old Testament and repeats it in the New Testament we can be sure that it applies to all time. It is being fulfilled in both the Old and New Covenants. It is for today.

The promise I have in mind is a vital one to our understanding of the full significance of forgiveness. It also provides the only definition of forgiveness that God is prepared to accept.

In the Old Testament it is found in Jeremiah 31:34, 'I will forgive their wickedness and will remember their sins no more.' The exact same promise is repeated in Hebrews 8:12.

It is hard enough to forgive, but surely it is impossible also to forget the deeds of the past. Is it not possible to completely forgive without having to forget as well? No one should be expected to forget.

In view of this problem about forgetting it is clearly important to find a correct understanding of this promise. First of all it is necessary to make a right distinction between forgetting something and not remembering it. This is not a case of splitting hairs. There is an important difference between the two.

The Lord does not promise to forget the deeds of the past.

If you forget something there is always a possibility that you will remember it again later on. If you forget where you left your spectacles, you hope very much that later in the day you will remember where you put them. What the Lord promises is: 'I will remember their sins no more.' To remember, according to my dictionary, means: 'To keep in mind, to recall to mind.' You keep the incident in your mind, to make sure that you do not forget it, and if it does slip out of your memory, you deliberately recall it to your mind. You are holding on to the sin that you need to forgive instead of letting it go out of your mind.

The Christian attitude should be to refuse to let the mind dwell on a sin once it has been forgiven. Every time something causes you to think of the incident, you put it out of your mind and refuse to dwell on it. You will not forget because things will happen to bring it back to your mind, but you will not deliberately dwell on the event or allow yourself to recall what happened. To put it from you whenever it comes back to mind is different from forgetting something completely.

Your biggest problem is that other people will keep reminding you of past hurts and want you to talk about them. When that happens it becomes a real struggle to refuse to allow your mind to entertain such thoughts. God must have this problem continuously. People keep talking to him in prayer about past faults and failings, all the things that God has long since forgiven. God does not have the same struggle over this that you or I would have. He just refuses to listen to us.

That is the only way that God could keep his promise to us: 'I will remember their sins no more.' He refuses to allow you to push such thoughts back into his mind. That may well be the very tactic that you and I will have to employ— to refuse to listen to people who try to drag up our past before us again. I wonder how many times you have prayed at length to the Lord about past events in your life without realizing that the Lord was not even listening to you. He is

133

faithful to his word to remember such things no more.

In Jeremiah 31:33–34 all of the pledges are on God's side. All the way through God is saying 'I will'. Our responsibility is to believe that God keeps his promises, that he does exactly what he says. If you have asked the Lord to forgive all your past sins then you must believe this promise. That is the only way in which you can be freed from all sense of guilt and go free in the liberty that forgiveness brings. Once you have confessed to God that you are a sinner in need of forgiveness, then it is up to you to remember those sins no more. God says, 'I will remember them no more.' You must do the same.

Can you imagine what this teaching meant to Peter? Three times he committed the sin of denying his Lord. He must have felt his life was ruined. He would never be of any use to God again. Then Jesus looked at him. Nothing was said. It was just a look, but how does Jesus look on a ruined life, or any ruined situation? 'The Lord will...look with compassion on all her ruins' (Isaiah 51:3). It was not a look of condemnation. It was a look of compassion. The result was Peter's tears. They signified his act of repentance, his cry of forgiveness.

When Peter and Jesus next met to talk together the Lord made not even the slightest reference to the sin of denial. The reason for this was that in his heart he had felt the sadness and repentance of Peter and had immediately forgiven him. That sin was now no longer in Jesus' memory. It had gone completely from his mind, and Peter was set free from all guilt for his sin.

Can you imagine what this teaching means to the nation of Israel? The nation that refused to recognize their Messiah when he came even though in his coming he fulfilled all of what they knew the Old Testament prophets foretold? It was a devastating denial of Jesus. It spelt out the ruination of themselves as a nation. But the Lord looks with compassion on ruins, and Jeremiah, who knew how to pronounce judgement on a people, nevertheless speaks the word of the

Lord when he says: 'I have loved you with an everlasting love' (31:3). Everlasting love produces eternal forgiveness and a mind that remembers sin no more. So God is able to say to the nation: 'Only if the heavens above can be measured and the foundations of the earth below be searched out will I reject all the descendants of Israel because of all they have done' (verse 37). The people of Israel have never been rejected by their God and today their nation has been restored to them. One day they will repent of their rejection of the Messiah, will see Jesus as Lord, and God will remember their sin no more.

Are you beginning to grasp what this teaching means to ordinary people like you and me, with all our faults and failings? As a man Jeremiah was no different from any other man. When he wrote the words we are considering, he was shut up in the court of the guard, a virtual prisoner. His faith was being tested to the limit. He was experiencing rejection by his own people and the word he spoke from the Lord was not being accepted. He was going through a difficult time, the sort of experience from which none of us can escape when once we are faithful in proclaiming God's word.

It is not easy to go to sleep at night when your mind is full of questions, when you cannot see clearly what God is doing, when you are beginning to doubt if you are in God's will at all. Then suddenly Jeremiah had a glorious night's sleep. It was a blessing no words could describe. All he could say was: 'At this I awoke and looked around. My sleep had been pleasant to me' (verse 26). When he looked around conditions were just the same, nothing had changed, he was still in custody, so how had he come to sleep so well? God had spoken. The silence had been broken. He had heard the words of assurance he needed, and fresh light had been thrown on his whole situation.

The Lord had dug up an old proverb that was often quoted in Jewish circles and he said there was a day coming when it would be no longer relevant. The saying would no longer be heard in the land. This is it: 'The Fathers have eaten sour grapes, and the children's teeth are set on edge' (verse 29). That proverb teaches that the sins of the past can influence the people of the present. One generation suffers from the sins of the previous generation. The Lord told Jeremiah that there was a day coming when that proverb would no longer be true.

That day has now come. The old proverb is no longer relevant. The doctrine of forgiveness means that the sins of the past are no longer remembered and therefore cannot influence the behaviour of the person who has learned how to forgive.

We must not allow our lives to be influenced by proverbs that are no longer true. We can, if we want, allow our lives to be governed by the past, but that does not have to be the case. Since Calvary's cross there has been a new law written on our hearts. It is the law of forgiveness. God told Jeremiah in this remarkable thirty-first chapter: 'This is the covenant that I will make with the house of Israel after that time,' declares the Lord. 'I will put my law in their minds and write it on their hearts. I will be their God, and they will be my people' (verse 33). In the next verse the Lord says that everyone will know him because he will forgive their wickedness and will remember their sin no more. Everything hinges on that act of forgiveness.

Jesus taught: 'Blessed are the pure in heart, for they will see God' (Matthew 5:8). To see God is to know him. Knowing God is possible for the pure in heart. Purity comes from the receiving and giving of full forgiveness, the kind that remembers no more.

This whole teaching is repeated by the writer of Hebrews. He goes through it all in chapter eight and carefully explains all the implications of such a glorious truth. He states: 'And where these have been forgiven, there is no longer any sacrifice for sin' (10:18). Christ's placing of his own life on the cross was such a perfect sacrifice that it achieves the kind of perfect forgiveness that remembers the sin no more.

Anything less than that is second-rate forgiveness. If a Christian forgives but deliberately remembers the sin committed he is denying the efficacy of Christ's sacrifice. It is as serious as that. Forgiveness is now a law written on the heart of every Christian and there is no escape from it, any more than there is any escape from the cross.

Before the cross sins were always remembered. 'Those sacrifices are an annual reminder of sins' (Hebrews 10:3). The one and only perfect sacrifice on the cross is to put the sin away from our remembrance for ever. We now remember Christ's death on the cross as we take the bread and wine but we do not, and must not, remember the sin that made the cross necessary. The cross is there to take away sin.

There are great implications in the cross but perhaps none greater than a proper understanding of this teaching of remembering sin no more.

13

'I Can Never Forgive'

Now we face up to the hard reality that there are thousands of people who have been hurt and who cannot forgive. I believe they are to be found in every congregation of Christian people.

I am not referring to those who are struggling hard to try to forgive. Those people, if they are sincere, will find the way of forgiveness. I am thinking of people who have decided that they cannot forgive. As you listen to them you realize the uncomfortable fact that they do not want to forgive.

Let us realize the fact that everyone we have met in this book has said: 'I cannot forgive.' The difference is that they have wanted to do what was humanly impossible and God has honoured that desire and has given them the gift of forgiveness. The people we are now considering have started from the same point of saying: 'I cannot forgive,' but the desire to forgive is not in their hearts. Listen to them carefully and the truth slowly dawns on you that what in fact they are saying is: 'I do not want to forgive.' They are fighting against and resisting any possibility that one day they might forgive. They want to rule that out completely.

A lady from Northern Ireland whose husband had been shot dead by terrorists sat down with me, as so many others have done, to share her experience. I had no idea how she was reacting. She was one of the scores of people whose lives have been brutally invaded by the horror of the murderer's bullets.

When I met this lady she had lived with this deep hurt for six years. She was not talking to me about first reactions, her initial response to the killing. The wound had been given time to heal. Her reaction now was a carefully thought out one. This was not a purely emotional response. It had been deliberately conceived.

She could look me straight in the eyes and tell me with all the honesty of her heart that she hated the man who had killed her husband. There was no attempt to shield from view the bitterness that was in her heart. It was there for all to see and there were moments when it showed in her eyes.

This was not an evil person with whom I was talking. Neither was she a hermit, hiding herself away to feed on her own bitterness all by herself. This was a woman with a very wide circle of friends who knew her as someone on whom they could always call for help. That is why it is so important to recognize this person, because her counterpart may be sitting in church next Sunday morning. It may not be murder that has caused the hatred. It may be a broken marriage or a promotion in the office that went to the wrong person. The person burning with hatred may be male or female, but the important factor to recognize is that they can be practising Christians.

Try to understand this person. Perhaps her reaction is the normal, natural one. Perhaps she is the true representative of the average person. The other people mentioned in this book may be the exceptions to the rule.

Look at her carefully. It is not often that she can be persuaded to sit down for so long to talk about herself. She is a tireless social worker, seeking no praise for what she is doing, but reaching out continuously to help old age pensioners, widows and the sick. Her good deeds would put other Christians to shame. The only thing missing from her life is the miracle of forgiveness.

She is glad that no one has been arrested for killing her husband. One day the police may trace the gun that fired the fatal shot, but there are no clues at all as to whose hand held the gun, whose finger pulled the trigger. This gives her the freedom to let her hatred range over a wide area. She can direct it wherever she likes, for anyone could be the killer. It sounds as though there are times when her hatred just gets lost somewhere in the air.

Just like the Athenians worshipped an unknown god, and even built an altar to the anonymous deity, so this lady is hating an unknown being. It is easier that way. If the killer is ever caught and identified she will have to focus all her hatred on to one person, and I think she would find that hard to do. An arrest could be the turning point in her life. It might start off a change in her attitude. At the moment she can extend her hatred in all directions, but in fact she is hating no one in particular. The only person feeling the hatred is herself.

Look at her again. This is not an unhappy woman. She can smile and laugh. She is enjoying the opportunities she has to help other people and gets satisfaction from such work. She is a likable and friendly person. She can hate without manifesting her hatred. Somewhere in Ireland there is a man waiting to receive forgiveness, but he may never receive it from her.

The situation is not without hope, however. Everyone is capable of change and she will admit that she too has changed, in one respect at least. There was a time after her husband's murder when she thought of all Roman Catholics as being supporters of the IRA. This was a blanket reaction on her part, extending to every member of the Catholic community. She preferred to have no contact with any of them. She looked with suspicion on everyone who entered a Catholic church. That is no longer her reaction. Time has brought about a change in her attitude. Today she has many Catholic friends. She is glad that this barrier has gone out of her life, and in some ways I think she is surprised at the extent to which her attitude has changed. There was a time when she did not think that such a change would ever be possible.

It was around this time in our conversation that she began to reveal that she has lost something of the reality of Christ's presence in her life. Her hatred had created a barrier between her and the Lord. We talked about that and how Christ could remove that barrier and become real to her. She could recognize that it was her hatred that had created the barrier between her and the Lord. But she did not want to let go of that hatred. I told her how the Lord could take it from her and she knew that this was true.

'I am not willing to give it up,' she said. 'It keeps me going. I do not think I could do without it now. It works up the adrenalin within me.'

As you read those words, almost able to hear her say them, you may be thinking of the reply you would give to that lady. We always want to come up with the answer. We are always quick to respond. We think it more important to answer people than we do to listen to them. It is only as we listen that we will discover what God is doing in their lives. He has the answer and it is very seldom the one that we would give.

I sat and listened. 'You tell me to let Christ deal with this hatred. I find myself drawing back from that possibility.' I still sat and listened because she had not yet revealed what her final response was going to be. She looked at me with a smile. 'I'll have to think about that,' she said.

I saw a couple of bricks fall from the wall that stood between her and Christ. She was open to think about what Christ could do in her life. She left me to disappear in the crowd again where she is so busy doing good to others. Do try to understand her. You may be more likely to come across people like her than you are to meet that smaller but growing number of people who have experienced a miracle in their lives—the gift of forgiveness.

Now let me introduce you to a man. He is an orthodox Jew and what he says about forgiveness would be echoed by most people who share his orthodox faith. He tells me that he cannot accept the Christian teaching on forgiveness and does not believe it to be the right theological line to take.

'There is no way that I can forgive the German people for what they did to the thousands of Jews who were murdered in the gas chambers. It would not be right for me to offer such forgiveness. The only people who could forgive are the Jews who died. There is no way that I could try to put myself in their shoes and offer a forgiveness that they may not want to give. It would be wrong for me to do so. I am therefore in the position that I can never forgive the German people for what they did and for what they allowed to happen.'

That is an interesting concept that needs to be understood aright. A Christian who finds himself in a similar position as that Jew may well begin to react in a similar way. The argument sounds persuasive. There have been many Christian martyrs over the centuries, people who were put to death for no other reason than that they held to the Christian faith. We cannot stand in their shoes. We stand on our own feet and judge the reactions of our own hearts. The Jew of today who feels resentment against the present generation of German people needs to repent of that reaction and to ask them for forgiveness.

There is a degree to which Christians can go further than that. I have seen a party of English Christians, including church leaders, attending a conference in the Republic of Ireland and embracing Irish Christians, asking their forgiveness for all the wrongs done in the past by England towards Ireland. I have seen the same reconciliation take place between Irish Catholics and Protestants. They were repenting for wrong attitudes in the present but also asking for forgiveness for all the hurts of the past. Such acts are unplanned. They take place spontaneously in an atmosphere of worship and adoration of Christ. There is an extent to which we all need to be freed from the hurts inherited from the deeds of previous generations.

Forgiveness has a wide sweep to it that is all-encompassing. There is a breadth to it that is all-embracing. There is a depth to it that can be measured only by comparing it to the depth of God's love.

14

A Miracle and a Gift

Having listened carefully to all the people interviewed for this book, and studied prayerfully the Scripture passages quoted, I am faced with two conclusions. To be able to receive and grant forgiveness is a miracle that cannot be experienced by human effort or willpower alone. Secondly, forgiveness is a gift for which we ask. We receive forgiveness as a gift and we ask for the gift of forgiveness so that we may forgive others.

These two factors come through very clearly to me as the main conclusions to be reached. Forgiveness is a miracle and forgiveness is a gift.

It is also clear that there is only one definition of forgiveness that is acceptable to the heart of God. That is the forgiveness which remembers sin no more. This is far superior to the forgiveness that the world has come so easily to accept. The world says: 'I forgive you, but I will never forget.' That comes nowhere near the forgiveness that God offers and expects us to give.

Whether forgiveness is accepted or rejected is not the important issue for the person who forgives. We must do more than offer forgiveness to a person. We must give forgiveness. It must leave us and go out to the person. We must know we have given that forgiveness and remember the sin no more. That is our responsibility. The other person's response is not our responsibility.

That is how God forgives. Forgiveness flows from the cross to every individual on the earth in every generation. God is constantly giving. The majority of people reject that forgiveness, but that is their responsibility.

Many people who receive God's forgiveness in all its fullness never ask for the gift of forgiveness to give to others. They never experience the miracle of being able to forgive and to remember the sin no more. The forgiveness they may offer people is a very shallow reflection of the real thing. It is full of remembrances that create bitterness and resentments.

This type of giving is seen in ways other than the act of forgiveness. It is seen in the proclamation of the word of God. Every Christian has the responsibility to proclaim the word, to give the gift of the truth of the gospel so that all may hear. The fact that in most cases the word will fall on stony ground or be choked by worries, riches or pleasures must never stop us from speaking it forth. Some will fall on good ground and be received. The reception of the word must never influence the degree to which we give it forth. The word is a gift too precious to withhold from people just because they may reject it.

The same is true of the role of the prophet. God gives the prophet a message to proclaim to the people. He must speak that word for all to hear even if they reject it to the extent of throwing him into prison to shut him up. If the prophet fails to give the message then he is held responsible for any judgement that falls on the people. So long as the prophet is faithful in giving the message, he is free of all responsibility as to how it is received.

This is made abundantly clear in the case of the prophet Jeremiah. It is hard to think of any other prophet whose message was rejected to the extent that Jeremiah's was, but he kept faithful to the task of giving it out to both the king and the people. It is more than offering the word. If you offer the word to someone and they say they do not want it, then you do not give it to them. The word must be given and then the hearer is forced to take action, to either accept or reject. Forgiveness is not something we offer and withdraw if it is not wanted. Forgiveness has to be given.

Christ, as always, is the perfect example of what it means to give even in the face of rejection. He gave, and kept on giving, until eventually he gave his life. From the moment of his resurrection he has never ceased to give.

Forgiveness is the new song that I hear coming from the hearts of more and more people. But it seems that the song is heard most clearly when it comes from those areas of the world where the suffering is greatest. It was in Northern Ireland that I first heard the song, but it was coming from the lives of people suffering from the murder of husbands or children. The forgiveness is bred in the hearts that have been most deeply hurt.

One reference to a new song is in the first verse of Psalm 149: 'Sing to the Lord a new song, his praise in the assembly of the saints.' That new song of forgiveness cannot be sung in the assembly of the saints if one person is withholding forgiveness from another. The assembly might try to sing the song, but it just would not ring true. But if ever a fellowship of Christians could be formed in which every person was a receiver and giver of true forgiveness, how glorious their new song would be. It would be sung in uninhibited grandeur, full-throated, a paean of praise ascending to the throne of God. Truly a new song to the Lord.

Christian leaders the world over who have put their thoughts on to paper have found it necessary, no matter with what subjects they may be dealing, to make some reference to the importance of forgiveness. Pastor John Wimber, director of Vineyard Ministries in the USA, whose teaching has influenced churches in many lands, has found that forgiveness plays an important part in the healing ministry of Christ and of the church. In his book, *Power Healing* (Hodder & Stoughton 1986), he states:

Jesus taught that unforgiveness will cause all types of personal torment on earth—spiritual, mental, emotional, physical and social. All of this culminates in eternity in hell. 'This is how my heavenly Father will treat each of you,' he said, 'unless you forgive your brother from your heart.' The principle is simple: God has given us mercy, so we may extend it to others, and if we forgive others we will continue to experience God's forgiveness.

The Scripture reference in that quotation is from Matthew 18:35, and the words were spoken by Jesus. He calls for forgiveness 'from your heart.' Forgiveness must never be simply an act of the will. True forgiveness has to be an experience of the heart, that is why it can be so costly and can even hurt to extend forgiveness to someone.

An American woman who has done a considerable amount of teaching in European countries is Leanne Payne. She has a wealth of experience in counselling people who have deep inner hurts. In her book *The Broken Image* (Crossway Books 1986) she states:

> There are three major barriers to inner healing and therefore to the maturity and wholeness of personality to which we are called. They are (1) failure to forgive others, (2) failure to receive forgiveness for ourselves, and (3) failure to accept and love ourselves aright.

I have listened to this woman teach and she is very strong on the view that unforgiveness creates a barrier in our lives that can hinder our whole spiritual growth and deny us the peace of mind and heart that God offers. Christ delights in breaking down all barriers that come between us and God and between ourselves and other people. But this particular barrier of unforgiveness can be removed only by our willingness to receive and to give forgiveness. The willingness is the essential quality. Once the willingness is there we can claim the miracle and the gift of forgiveness.

The barrier that unforgiveness can create seems to apply to almost every subject in life. Imagine lending someone a book or a cassette, expecting them to return it when they had finished with it. In fact you never get it back so you become critical of the person who borrowed and failed to return. That critical spirit of unforgiveness creates its own barrier in the situation and can actually prevent the return of what was borrowed.

Gene Lilly wrote of this happening in his book *God Is Calling His People to Forgiveness* (Marshall Morgan & Scott 1984). He asked his wife why people had suddenly started returning the books and tapes they had borrowed. I quote his wife's reply from the book:

> 'You remember when you were preaching on forgiveness the other day?' I nodded. 'You mentioned that Jesus said to lend, expecting nothing in return!' Again I nodded. 'Well, I prayed and forgave each and every person who had failed to return things they had borrowed,' she said. 'When I forgave them, it must have released them. I must have had them bound by my complaining against them!'
>
> What a truth she had learned about forgiveness! Now I could understand what had been going on. Now I understood why all the tapes and books had suddenly started flowing back. Unforgiveness had stopped up the channel but forgiveness had unclogged the pipes.

If that seems far-fetched, it is a principle that may be very easily put to the test. Nearly everyone has given something out on loan. If it has not come back, try forgiving the person who has not returned the article and see what happens. Such a simple experience could help us to see how unforgiveness can bind people and prevent them from doing the right thing while forgiveness can release them and set them free.

The Rev. Dr George Lovell, a Methodist minister, suffered the experience of finding his wife seriously injured and a close friend killed by a terrorist bomb placed in the Tower of London in 1974. He writes of what it means to remember that tragedy:

148

I have to remember in a mature way. For me this involves forgiveness, which is caught up in a correct approach to remembering. One of the sicknesses in the Irish situation is a highly elaborate cultic form of remembering—the deaths of the past, the martyrs, the atrocities.

This is a denial of the central act of remembrance of the Christian faith called by some the Mass, by others the Eucharist, by yet more Communion, where there is death, sin, bloodiness to the Son of God, now institutionalised and celebrated in such a way that it does not bring violence and hate but peace—shalom. (The Forgiveness and Politics Study Pack, 2 Eaton Gate, London SW1.)

You can always argue with a theologian— until you find one like this man who is speaking from experience and not just from theory. He has successfully married his theology, the theology of the Eucharist, to his terrible experience. He has discovered what is meant by remembering and by remembering no more. At the Lord's table we remember the supreme act of violence that for ever eradicates all bitterness and resentment from the remembrance of past sins, including those that were violent in nature.

Another theologian to speak on the subject is Dr Jerry Horner, Dean of the School of Biblical Studies at CBN University, Virginia, USA. In his book *Living in the Family* (Lamp Press, Georgia) he writes:

Jesus also said, 'If you do not forgive men, then your Father will not forgive your transgressions' (Matthew 6:15). The horrible sin of unforgiveness is a blight upon our Christian life that can rob us of the joy of the Lord. It can block the free flow of communion with the Lord and can embitter all of the relationships of life.

One of America's finest poets was Edwin Markham. At one period in his life he lost his inspiration and could not compose poetry. What had happened was that he had been terribly wronged by a business partner. Unable to forgive the man for the hurt inflicted upon him, Markham brooded over the wrong until his bitterness robbed him of the ability to write. Finally,

God's grace enabled him to express forgiveness for the man who had cheated him. In the vast relief which engulfed him upon forgiving his former partner, Markham sat down and wrote his famous couplet entitled 'Outwitted':

> He drew a circle that shut me out,
> Heretic, rebel, a thing to flout.
> But love and I had the wit to win,
> For we drew a circle that took him in.

There are two points in particular that impress me in this quotation. Dr Horner refers to 'the horrible sin of unforgiveness'. There is a need for every Christian to accept that the failure to forgive is a sin in the sight of God. Whether we consider the sin horrendous or just ordinary, it is still a sin. The acceptance of that fact will drive us to confess the sin and seek forgiveness from God, and that can be the first step towards us asking for the ability to forgive.

Secondly, there is the reference to God's grace that enabled him to express forgiveness. This is yet one more indication that the ability to forgive is a gift for which we must ask—it comes only by the grace of God.

The quotation also shows once again what a great blockage unforgiveness causes in our lives. The whole flow of inspiration ceased. The sin of unforgiveness can stop the free flow of the Holy Spirit in expressing his fruit and his gifts, and also stem the ability to expound freely the Scriptures under the anointing of the same Holy Spirit.

Now let us look at the teaching of an English cleric, the Rev. Ken Gardiner, vicar of St Philip and St James' in Kent. In his book *Watch This Space* (Kingsway Publications 1987) he states:

When Christ prayed for those who were nailing him to the cross, 'Father, forgive them, they don't know what they are doing,' those men did not deserve forgiveness. Christ prayed that prayer because of the person he was, not the people they were. He was free of all hatred and bitterness. Had he harboured hurt and unforgiveness that would have affected the person he was, just as harbouring such feelings affects us. We cannot be healed while we are bound by any unforgiveness on our part. Christ taught us to pray, 'Forgive us our sins as we forgive those who sin against us.' He knew the consequences for us, if we do not. I am not pretending such forgiveness is easy, I'm simply stating that it is essential.

In this teaching the barrier created by unforgiveness is in the ministry of healing. The failure to forgive can block the whole process of healing coming to our lives. All of these quotations are revealing what a serious subject forgiveness is.

On the negative side unforgiveness is a barrier to any form of spiritual growth. On the positive side forgiveness is a miracle that releases the free flow of God's love and power through our lives.

So we are back to our new song. Take up the vision of the psalmist who sang: 'Sing to the Lord a new song; sing to the Lord, all the earth' (Psalm 96:1). There is no limitation to that vision. It is of 'all the earth' singing a new song to the Lord. If that new song had the theme of 'I forgive...' What a transformation there would be in all the earth. What a profound effect this would have on world politics. Herein lies a road that could lead to international peace. Perhaps that is a vision that has to be left until Christ returns and establishes his kingdom on the earth.

How far can our vision extend for this new song to be heard? In every nation of the world there are people who should be able to sing this refrain. Look at another call that the psalmist makes: 'Sing to the Lord a new song, for he has done marvellous things; his right hand and his holy arm have worked salvation for him' (Psalm 98:1). Here the vision is for everyone who has experienced the marvellous work of God in providing salvation. They are the people of every nation who should be able to sing the new song. They have received forgiveness from God through the act of salvation, and so they should be wanting to give forgiveness as a gift to others. There are Christian people in every nation on the earth. If they were all singing this new song what a glorious freeing there would be throughout the world. People would be released from the bondages that are imposed by the sin of unforgiveness.

It is not surprising to find the new song being sung in heaven, around the throne. There it is extolling the worthiness of Christ (Revelation 5:9). Christ is worthy of all the honour we can bring to his name, but how dishonouring it is when we refuse the gift of forgiveness he gives to us. Christ died to make forgiveness a possibility for everyone to receive and to give. To reject his gift is tantamount to spitting on his face at the crucifixion. It would be a rejection of everything for which he lived and died.

When we accept God's forgiveness and then give that same gift to someone else, then we are singing with the heavenly beings. The act of forgiveness creates a new song that is worthy to be sung around the throne.

There is a new song that only a limited number of people will be able to sing and it would appear that they are the ones who pass through the great tribulation without losing their faith in God. It is said that: 'No-one could learn the song except the 144,000 who had been redeemed from the earth' (Revelation 14:3). That made me wonder if the new song of forgiveness could be sung only by those people who have suffered most cruelly from the violence of the world. Certainly they are the people I first heard singing the song. On the other hand I have never met anyone who sincerely wanted the gift of forgiveness and did not receive it, thereby having the new song put into their heart. The gift, and therefore the song, is not limited to those who suffer most severely. It is available to all, and at some stage in our lives we all need to forgive.

My advice therefore is: listen for the new song of forgiveness. You are most likely to hear it where the suffering has been greatest, but listen for it from everyone and, above all, let it create an echo in your own heart as you enter into the joy of forgiveness.

Hands Free of Violence

by J. Eric Mayer

Many would say that the gun rules in Northern Ireland. The people featured in this book used to believe it, and acted accordingly. But now it is Christ they hail as King. And they risk their lives to uphold that claim.

Whether it's a public apology to a prison officer; living with the prospect of reprisals; or refusing to allow sectarian differences to drive a wedge between brothers in Christ: such things call for resources beyond human courage alone. These true stories are a living testimony to the power of God not only to change lives but also to sustain and enable those he calls.

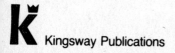

Kingsway Publications

Triumph Over Terror
on Flight 847

by Capt. John Testrake

'I taxied down the runway . . . his cocked pistol held against my head. In his other hand he held a grenade, with its pin pulled, directly in front of my face.'

Athens to Rome: it had promised to be a routine flight. But when two young men, armed and desperate, burst into the cockpit of his 727 plane, Captain John Testrake knew that every ounce of his professionalism and his faith were going to be called into action.

Very quickly his plane became the scene of harassment, abuse and even death, as the world looked on and held its breath. Yet strangely it was now that Captain Testrake discovered a profound sense of peace, a state of mind that would ultimately lead him out of the jaws of terrorism and also offer an answer to the fear and hatred that grip so much of today's terror-struck world.

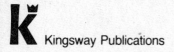

Kingsway Publications

Blood Brothers

by **Elias Chacour** *with David Hazard*

'The Jews and Palestinians are brothers, blood brothers,' said father. 'We share the same father—Abraham—and the same God. We must never forget that.'

Despite his father's words of peace, Elias Chacour sensed even as a child that enmity and mistrust were not so easily overcome.

Once Christian and Jew had shared the simple things of life together. But 1948 changed all that. The Zionists came, and almost a million Palestinians were made homeless. An exile in his own land, Elias faced the horrors of violence when tens of thousands lost their lives.

Then his father, his brother, and most of the village men disappeared.

In the years that followed, Elias struggled to find a way of peace that would avoid violence and yet accomplish more than his father's passive attitude. Then, just as he was about to begin a quiet life of service to the church, he received a new and dangerous calling that would take him right through the world's most bitter conflict.

A way of hope and reconciliation beckoned.

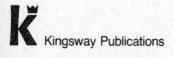

Kingsway Publications